SHERRILL KAHN

CREATING

Martingale & Company

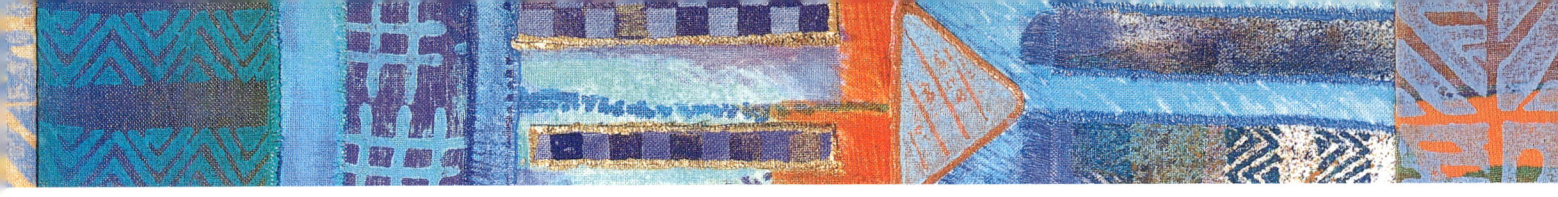

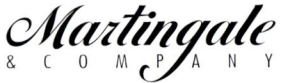

BOTHELL, WASHINGTON

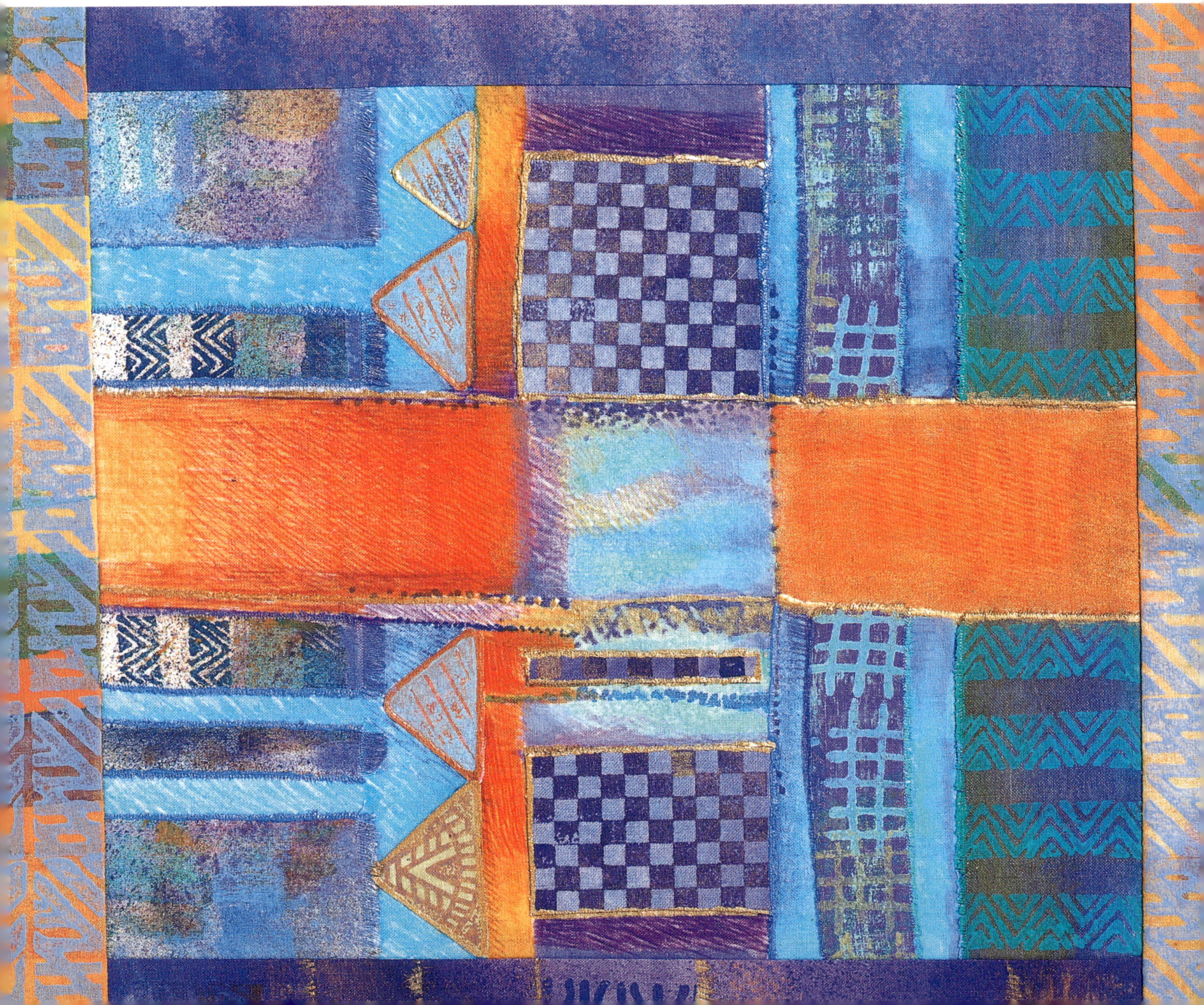

with PAINT

New Ways, New Materials

Creating with Paint: New Ways, New Materials

© 2001 by Sherrill Kahn

Martingale & Company
PO Box 118
Bothell, WA 98041-0118 USA
www.patchwork.com

Martingale
& COMPANY

That Patchwork Place is an imprint of Martingale & Company.

Printed in China
06 05 04 03 02 01   6 5 4 3 2 1

No part of this product may be reproduced in any form, unless otherwise stated, in which case reproduction is limited to the use of the purchaser. The written instructions, photographs, designs, projects, and patterns are intended for the personal, noncommercial use of the retail purchaser and are under federal copyright laws; they are not to be reproduced by any electronic, mechanical, or other means, including informational storage or retrieval systems, for commercial use. Permission is granted to photocopy patterns for the personal use of the retail purchaser.

The information in this book is presented in good faith, but no warranty is given nor results guaranteed. Since Martingale & Company has no control over choice of materials or procedures, the company assumes no responsibility for the use of this information.

Library of Congress Cataloging-in-Publication Data

Kahn, Sherrill,
  Creating with paint : new ways, new materials / author Sherrill Kahn.
    p. cm.
  ISBN 1-56477-320-5
  1. Painting. 2. Decoration and ornament. I. Title.
TT385 .K34 2001
745.7'23—dc21
                                            00-048059

MISSION STATEMENT

We are dedicated to providing quality products and service by working together to inspire creativity and to enrich the lives we touch.

CREDITS

President • Nancy J. Martin
CEO • Daniel J. Martin
Publisher • Jane Hamada
Editorial Director • Mary V. Green
Editorial Project Manager • Tina Cook
Technical Editors • Dawn Anderson
& Karen Soltys
Copy Editor • Liz McGehee
Design Director • Stan Green
Cover and Text Designer • Trina Stahl
Illustrator • Laurel Strand
Photographer • Brent Kane

DEDICATION

To my loving husband, Joel. For almost thirty-four years, he has been my best friend, mentor, and hero. Without his support, encouragement, invaluable ideas, and help, this book would not have been completed. I feel lucky to have such a special person enriching my life.

ACKNOWLEDGMENTS

I would like to thank my editor, Dawn Anderson, for her invaluable help and suggestions. Her clear insight helped me to organize this book logically. I would also like to thank Terry Martin for her encouragement and support. Brent Kane is a genius behind the camera lens. Thank you, Brent. I also want to thank my designer, Trina Stahl; art director Stan Green; and everyone at Martingale & Company who helped make this book possible. I appreciate your outstanding efforts.

Thanks to my dear sister, Anjani, for her constant loving support. To all of my many teachers, thank you so much for the knowledge that you gave to me. And finally, thank you to my friends and family—you make my life so rich. I will be forever grateful to all of you. Dad and Mom, I hope that you are watching in heaven. And last but not least, Sharilyn Miller—you got me here—thank you, thank you, thank you!

CONTENTS

INTRODUCTION • 8

GETTING STARTED • 10

    Painting Surfaces • 11

    Paints and Coloring Agents • 13

    Tools • 18

    Workspace • 19

    Preparing to Paint • 20

    Cleaning Up • 21

    Storing Painted Pieces • 21

SPONGE PAINTING • 22

    Basic Sponging • 23

    Dry Sponging • 24

    Sponging Repeat Patterns • 25

    Pop-Up Sponges • 26

    Sponging over Mesh • 28

    Washes • 29

    Wet into Wet • 30

    Scrunched Wet into Wet • 32

    Salt Textures • 33

    Plastic Wrap Patterns • 34

RUBBER STAMPING • 36

    Rubber Stamping with Paint • 38

    Rubber Stamping with Ink Pads • 40

TECHNIQUES FOR ALTERNATIVE TOOLS • 42

    Applicator-Tipped Paint Techniques • 43

    Ink Bleed with Markers • 45

    Credit Card Techniques • 47

    Toothbrush Spatter • 48

    Brayers • 50

    Techniques for Texture Tools • 52

RESISTS • 54

    Paint Resists • 55

    Crayon Batik • 55

    Tape Resists • 58

    Freezer-Paper Resists • 60

    Gels and Modeling-Paste Resists • 62

PRINTMAKING WITHOUT A PRESS · 64

Monoprints · 65

String Prints · 67

Bubble-Wrap Prints · 68

Foam-Plate Prints · 69

COMBINING THE TECHNIQUES · 72

Creating a Rich Painted Surface in Five Easy Steps · 73

GALLERY · 76

Boxes · 76

Dolls · 77

Books · 78

Necklaces · 80

Vests · 81

Glass, Ceramic, and Plastic Art Pieces · 82

Wall Hangings · 84

VEST · 85

DOLL · 88

WALL HANGING · 92

JOURNAL · 96

WOOD FRAME · 100

CERAMIC MUG · 102

GLASS · 104

METAL BASKET · 106

RESOURCES · 108

ABOUT THE AUTHOR · 110

INTRODUCTION

Do you **remember** the first time you painted? You probably used your **fingers** and found that you loved the **sensation** of applying **paint** to paper. As you grew older, you might have used brushes or sponges, but it still was a **wonderful** sensation. Try to remember the **innocence** of that early experience and try to capture the feeling of **joy** that you felt when using paint for the first time.

THIS BOOK SHOWS you simple techniques that are fun and easy to do. These techniques expand the creative possibilities of a variety of tools, materials, and paint, and work on a multitude of surfaces. You can use paper, wood, cloth, clay, cardboard, walls, canvas, glass, metal, ceramics, leather, or any other material that comes to mind. I hope this book will be used by teachers, artists, fiber artists, ceramists, young children, or anyone else who loves to play with art materials.

As you work, constantly ask yourself "What if?" You will amaze yourself at how experimenting will lead to wonderful results. Don't worry about creating a masterpiece; just have fun. You will find the hours fly by as you enjoy the pure pleasure of putting paint onto your chosen surface.

I have always loved art and, from an early age, decided that what I would love most is to teach art. My parents felt that teaching elementary school would be better, but after one semester of elementary education courses, I went back to the art department to pursue my dream of teaching art in secondary schools. I taught fine art, crafts, and design for the Los Angeles Unified School District for thirty years. It was a rewarding and fulfilling experience. Three years after retiring, my husband, Joel, and I started our own rubber stamp company called Impress Me. I draw all of the rubber stamp images, using ethnic art and petroglyphs for my inspiration. The rubber stamps used throughout this book are from our little rubber stamp company. I found that stamping opened up new painting horizons and added an incredible tool to my paint box.

I'm still teaching, sharing the myriad ideas possible with a little paint and creativity. The techniques and samples offered in this book are the result of these wonderful teaching experiences. Have fun!

GETTING STARTED

You will **discover** that many of the tools and supplies suggested for the various **techniques** shown in this book are already in your home. It is not necessary to purchase expensive art supplies. This book is intended to **inspire** and **encourage** experimentation.

THE TECHNIQUES SHOWN in this book work on a variety of surfaces, including paper, fabric, wood, ceramic, glass, metal, plastic, leather, canvas, walls, stone, or any other surface that will accept paint. Many of the samples shown in this book have been done on fabric; however, most of the techniques can be used on other surfaces, as long as you use the appropriate paint. Experimenting will yield important information about which surface works best for each technique.

Each section has its own supply list; however, you should refer back to this section for supplies used repeatedly throughout the book. Since the projects are intended for people of all ages and abilities, all supplies used should be nontoxic. Look for "nontoxic" displayed prominently on labels when choosing paints and inks.

Remember: ask yourself "What if?" as you try the techniques. The most important thing is to have fun!

PAINTING SURFACES

Fabric

I used quilting-quality muslin for most of the fabric samples in this book. You can use a wide variety of other fabrics since the paint is pigment based. Pigment-based paints sit on the surface of the fabric and aren't absorbed into the fibers the way dyes are.

Prewashing fabric is a personal decision. I do not prewash my fabric. The crisp fabric is appealing to me when I am working with it, and the paint seems to adhere to it very well. For best results, press the fabric well with a steam iron to remove all wrinkles before painting.

Paper

All of the techniques shown in this book work beautifully on paper. Cover-weight (or card-stock) paper from paper-supply stores works especially well. You can purchase it by the sheet, and it's often inexpensive. Watercolor paper is also an excellent choice for painting on paper because it buckles less than lightweight papers. Choose a paper that is at least 60 pounds or more for better results when using a lot of water. Paper that is lighter than 60 pounds often buckles when wet. The

If you want to paint it, no matter what the surface, chances are you can find the right paint for the job.

exception to this is sandwich paper, which is formulated to resist heavy moisture. Lighter-weight papers, such as computer paper, typing paper, rice paper, or specialty papers may be used for stamping with rubber stamp pads or for working with dry materials. Try a variety of papers and compare the results. All of the painting techniques shown in this book can also be used on cardboard or mat board. The surface of the cardboard or mat board will affect the outcome of the painted piece. Foam-core board will also take paint beautifully.

Sandwich paper, found at restaurant-supply stores, can be used in a variety of ways. It takes painting, sponging, and stamping beautifully. I like to use it for covering my work surface, especially when working with wet fabric techniques. The paint bleeds through the fabric onto the sandwich paper, leaving gorgeous painted designs on the paper once it is dry. Save the paint-stained sandwich paper to use later in paper projects, such as collage, greeting cards, or for interior pages in handmade books. Sandwich paper is also water-resistant and can be used for heat-setting fabric. Buy sandwich paper that is flat, not folded, in economical sizes, since you will use vast quantities of it in your work.

Wood

Wood offers an ideal painting and stamping surface. Look for ready-to-paint wood products at craft stores. Lightly sand the wood if it has not been presanded. Use a clean, slightly damp cloth to remove the sanding dust. Pretreating your wood project with a sealer depends on the result you wish to achieve. Experiment on scrap wood to determine whether you want to pretreat the surface. After finishing the project, sealing the wood is important, especially if the wood will be exposed to weathering. Wood sealers compatible with the paint you have used are available where paints are sold.

Glass and Ceramic

Many new paint products are available for painting on glass and prefired ceramics. Painted glass and ceramic pieces make wonderful gifts. Choose plain glass or ceramic for decorating. Colored ceramic pieces will also work. If choosing dark ceramic pieces, use contrasting opaque colors for the most effective results. Transparent ceramic colors don't work well on dark backgrounds. The most effective painting techniques for glass and ceramic are sponging, painting with a brush, decorating with permanent markers, and rubber stamping.

Ceramic tiles offer another wonderful paint surface. Tiles already in place in the kitchen and bathroom may be decorated with air-cured paint (paint that doesn't need to be heat-set in an oven). Tiles that are not yet installed can be decorated with your choice of oven-cured paints.

Plastic

The paint products used to decorate glass and ceramics can also be used on plastic. You cannot bake plastic in the oven, so air-cured products must be used. Permanent markers work beautifully on plastic. My friend Jacqui Wou introduced me to painting touch, or tap, lights. They are economical to buy, fun to paint and decorate, and beautiful when lit. The most effective painting techniques for plastic are sponging, painting with a brush, rubber stamping, and drawing with permanent markers.

Metal

Metal offers a unique surface for painting. Anything made from metal can be sponged, stamped, and painted. Use paints especially designed for painting on metal and follow the manufacturer's directions for pretreating and sealing the metal. Experiment with different techniques to find out which works best for each creative project.

Leather

Real and synthetic leather and suede come in many weights, finishes, and colors. Because leather does not ravel, it is an outstanding surface for creative projects. It can be combined with metal, wood, paper, and cloth to create wearables, wall hangings, dolls, jewelry, handmade books, and more. Leather can be rubber stamped, painted, and sponged. Experiment on scrap pieces before tackling larger projects.

PAINTS AND COLORING AGENTS

Acrylics

Acrylic paints come in bottles, tubes, and jars in a wide color range, including metallic, pearlescent, and interference colors, and can be used on almost any surface. They may be used full strength or diluted with water or a variety of paint mediums. Each medium has a specific purpose. Experiment to discover what acrylic mediums can do. For example, acrylics painted directly on fabric tend to be stiff. Adding a textile medium to the paint can give the fabric a softer feel. Fabrics painted with acrylics that have been mixed with a textile medium require heat-setting (see "Heat-Setting Fabric Paints" on page 14). For best results, follow the manufacturer's instructions when using textile mediums.

Acrylic modeling pastes and gels are fantastic for creating textured surfaces for painting. These pastes and gels may be colored with acrylic paints before applying them to the paint surface. Experiment with combining different acrylic paints, mediums, and pastes for interesting effects. Keep notes on your experiments.

A wide assortment of acrylic paints, ink pads, and permanent markers are available for your craft projects. Choose the coloring agent most suitable for the surface you are painting.

GETTING STARTED 13

Jar Acrylics

Jar acrylics are very thick. Use a plastic spoon or a wooden craft stick to apply paint from a jar to the palette. Or use a brush or sponge to pick up paint on the inside of the lid. Jar paint can be used for any of the techniques shown in this book. It must be diluted with water when creating washes (see "Washes" on page 29). I recommend Golden jar acrylics.

Tube Acrylics

Tube acrylic paint can be squeezed directly onto the palette. Dilute the paint with water from an eyedropper and mix with a brush before using it on your project. Diluted tube paint can be used for all painting techniques. I recommend Golden tube acrylics.

Bottled Acrylics

Bottled acrylics are thick enough to use for stamping (see "Rubber Stamping" on page 36) and painting details without dilution, and can be thinned with water for washes. Bottled acrylics are the most economical acrylics available. I recommend Delta Ceramcoat, DecoArt Americana, and Folk Art acrylic color by Plaid. They all offer a wide color assortment, including metallic colors.

Heat-Setting Fabric Paints

Fabric paint must be heat-set for permanence according to the manufacturer's instructions. It is preferable to heat-set the fabric forty-eight hours or more after painting. Acrylic paint does not have to be heat-set unless a fabric medium has been added to it.

To heat-set fabric paint:

1. Cover the ironing board with waterproof sandwich paper, special Teflon for heat-setting, or parchment paper. Set the iron to a temperature that corresponds to the type of fabric used. Steam helps heat-set the paint.

2. Place the fabric facedown on the ironing board. If it is badly wrinkled, spray water on it before ironing.

3. Press the piece well, allow to dry, then store it flat. Because many of the fabric pieces I paint are rather small, I use resealable plastic bags for storing all of my painted fabrics.

Liquid Acrylics

Liquid acrylics are packaged in bottles. Golden makes an incredible liquid acrylic called Golden Fluid Acrylic. It is highly pigmented and thin enough for painting small details with a brush. The color intensity makes it versatile for painting on all surfaces. Dr. Ph. Martin's also makes an excellent liquid acrylic called Spectralite.

Water-Based House Paints

Water-based, or latex, house paint is similar to acrylic paint and can be substituted for acrylic paints when economy is important. It can be used for many of the techniques shown in this book. House paints are ideal for working with children, scout troops, campcraft programs, and other situations where inexpensive materials are needed.

Fabric Paints

Fabric paint works beautifully for most fabric surfaces. It will not dry stiff like acrylics do. Fabric paint usually comes in jars and squeeze bottles. Fabric paints from jars work well for rubber stamping because they are usually thick. Use a wooden craft stick or a plastic spoon to place the color on the palette. An alternative is to dip a sponge or a brush into the paint found on the inside of the lid. Colors can be used singly or applied to the palette on top of one another for color richness. Fabric paint from squeeze bottles is often more liquid than fabric paint from jars. Liquid fabric paint works well for washes. I recommend Jacquard Lumiere and Jacquard Textile Color, Pebeo Setacolor, Tulip Ultra Soft, Createx Multi-Surface Acrylic, Ranger Rubber Stamp Fabric Paint, and Dr. Ph. Martin's ReadyTex bottled fabric paint. Heat-set all fabric paint according to the manufacturer's instructions.

Applicator-Tipped Paints

Applicator-tipped paints are primarily used for outlining areas of interest. They can be used to create textural areas by dragging scraping tools through the paint. Scraping tools can be items such as old credit cards, plastic knives and forks, and tools used to apply tile adhesive. Dilute applicator-tipped paints for washes (see "Washes" on page 29). I recommend Tulip by Duncan, Jones Tones, and Plaid applicator-tipped paints.

These paints don't require heat-setting when used on fabric (see "Heat-Setting Fabric Paints" on page 14), but if they are used in conjunction with another paint that must be heat-set, wait at least 24 to 48 hours before heat-setting. Cover your ironing board and the project with sandwich paper or parchment paper before heat-setting applicator-tipped paint. If you forget to do this step, the paint could stick to your iron or ironing board and you could possibly destroy your iron and your creation.

GETTING STARTED 15

Pigment-Based Dyes for Fabric

Pigment-based dyes are manufactured for use on fabric. They are similar to silk dyes and can be heat-set with an iron. I recommend Jacquard's Dye-na-Flow, and Pebeo's Setasilk pigment-based dyes. Dr. Ph. Martin's ReadyTex fabric paints act similarly to dyes and are highly pigmented.

Watercolors

Watercolors work beautifully for most of the techniques shown in this book. Since watercolor is not permanent, watercolor pieces are best preserved by framing behind glass. I recommend Dr. Ph. Martin's Hydrus watercolors.

Rubber Stamp Pads

Many types of rubber stamp pads are available at craft and rubber stamp stores. There are pigment-based stamp pads and dye-based stamp pads. Each has different properties. Experiment with different stamp-pad inks to find the effect you prefer. Some are made specifically for fabric. Fabric stamped with fabric ink must be heat-set. Read the manufacturer's instructions before using the stamp pad and take notes on your creative endeavors. I recommend Ranger, Clearsnap, Dr. Ph. Martin's, and Tsukineko rubber stamp pads.

Inks

Inks work best on paper or other surfaces that do not need to be heat-set. Inks are transparent and some are waterproof. Layers of colors can be painted, creating rich, dramatic effects. Experiment to discover the brand of ink that you like best. I recommend Dr. Ph. Martin's Bombay India Ink.

Metal Paints

A number of paints work very well on metal. Check with your local craft store and experiment with different products to see which works best for your project. I recommend Dr. Ph. Martin's Metal Craft, Delta Perm Enamel, Deco Art's metal paint or Ultra Gloss, and Plaid's Indoor and Outdoor Gloss paint. Follow the manufacturer's directions when using metal paints. Some paints require that a metal primer be used first.

This tin can was sponged and rubber stamped with Dr. Ph. Martin's Metacraft paint. Details were painted with a small, flat brush. An element made of cloth, wire, and seed beads was added to the can with wire.

Glass and Ceramic Paints

Painting on glass and prefired ceramics has become very popular, and you'll find a number of glass and ceramic paints available in craft stores. Most glass paints will also work on plastic. Many glass and ceramic paints are permanently set by firing them in the oven, and some can be air-cured or sealed with a liquid glaze. Follow the manufacturer's instructions when using these products. Only some brands of glass and ceramic paints are safe for contact with food, so it is important to read the label before purchasing the paint to check the manufacturer's recommendations. For glass painting, I prefer Delta's Textured Gel and Transparent Glass paint, Pebeo's Vitrea, and Plaid's Gallery Glass. For ceramics, I recommend Delta's Perm Enamel, Pebeo's Porcelaine 150, Deco Art's Ultra Gloss, and Plaid's Apple Barrel Gloss Enamel.

Markers

Markers are an easy way to add color to any project. Each marker has unique properties. The color range in markers is extensive and there are also a number of tip sizes to choose from. Metallic markers, gel rollers, and other new products constantly expand the products available for creative endeavors. Sanford's Sharpie pens are permanent and work well on plastic, glass, and ceramics. Experiment to find out which markers work best for your projects.

Colored Pencils

Colored pencils provide a clean and easy way to add color to rubber-stamped and painted pieces. Some colored pencils are very waxy and highly pigmented and others are harder and less pigmented, so experimenting is essential when working with colored pencils. Build the colors slowly and gradually, layer upon layer, for more interesting pieces. Colored pencil lines can add wonderful accents to finished pieces. I recommend Prismacolor pencils.

This pin was rubber stamped, stuffed, and embellished with seed beads.

GETTING STARTED 17

TOOLS

Rubber Stamps

Rubber stamps can be wonderful tools in your creative process. All of the rubber stamps used in this book are from Impress Me, the company my husband and I started in 1996. I hand draw all of the designs, and many are inspired by ethnic sources. We are an angel company, meaning that all designs hand stamped with our images can be sold. The stamps are very deeply etched and unmounted. They can be used on any surface and cleaned with water and a toothbrush at the end of the creative process. You can use other rubber stamps as well. Caution should be used when cleaning paint from mounted stamps to avoid damaging the stamps.

Paint Palette

Artist's acrylic and oil painting strip palettes work well for mixing paints. You can purchase strip palettes at an art-supply or a craft store, or you can create your own palette from freezer paper. Cut the paper into 12" squares and roll the cut sheets in the opposite direction of the natural roll to flatten them. Use the shiny side of the paper for your palette.

Sponges

Most of the samples in this book were created from hydrophilic sponges that never harden, available at hardware stores and lumberyards. Other sponges will work, but these sponges are excellent. They are usually dark yellow and the edges are rounded. Large hydrophilic sponges are 7¼" long by 5" wide, and about 2" thick. I cut them with Fiskars Soft-Touch shears or heavy scissors into smaller sizes, about 1½" x 1½". Smaller sponge squares are handy for painting tiny areas.

Brushes

Brushes are great for painting solid areas of color, applying washes (see "Washes" on page 29), or painting details. I prefer flat brushes for painting washes, and round brushes for painting details. Choose the brush size that works best for the technique you are doing. When applying paint with flat brushes, hold the brush perpendicular to the surface, and you'll find it easy to blend colors and fade painted edges. I recommend Plaid synthetic brushes.

Heat Gun

Heat guns speed the paint-drying process. I prefer the Ranger Heat It craft tool and use it frequently when producing a variety of artwork.

Although a variety of tools can be used for creative painting, only a few are necessary. Some I use most often are shown here.

Water Containers

Keep one or more large water containers handy when working on your creative project. You will need the water for wet techniques such as "Washes" and "Wet into Wet" as well as for cleaning your brushes and rubber stamps.

Cutting Tools

You will need scissors for cutting paper and fabric. Paper cutters are also invaluable tools, especially if paper is your primary paint surface. If possible, have a small paper cutter handy for cutting various paper sizes. Fiskars makes a portable model, which stores easily. If space allows, an additional traditional paper cutter would be ideal. A 15" paper cutter will handle most paper-cutting jobs. For detailed paper cutting, you may also want to have a sharp craft knife. For cutting fabric, rotary cutters, rulers, and self-healing mats are invaluable. Tearing fabric is another option.

WORKSPACE

It would be ideal to have a creative workspace that could be set up permanently. If a permanent space is not possible, there are many alternatives—including making space in a closet. The minimum work surface you will need is 3 feet by 3 feet, but a bigger space is even better. To keep your work surface uncluttered, place a rolling cart or television tray adjacent to your work area to hold more supplies.

You can create a simple and inexpensive work surface with a door purchased from a lumberyard. Paint and seal the door before using it. Place the door on top of two or three plastic or wooden storage containers with drawers. The result will be a long work surface with an opening for seating.

A rolling plastic cart with a number of different-sized drawers is ideal for holding art supplies. The drawers are removable and can be placed on the work surface. Wire bins and plastic containers are also ideal for holding supplies. They stack easily and can be brought to the work surface when needed.

When filling the storage drawers or bins, put similar products together. Place the crayons, pencils, and other dry media in one drawer. Place the brushes, sponges, and other tools for applying paint in another. By arranging your drawers according to the supplies in them, you can locate your supplies easily.

I use a swivel chair when working, since it lets me move in and out of my work area easily. Be sure to select a chair that is comfortable and supports your back.

Recording Details

Keep a notebook and permanent pen handy when working on painting experiments. Jot down the method used to create the sample or painting, so it will be easy to repeat the process at a future date. You can also label individual pieces with a permanent marker and keep the samples in a binder in plastic sleeves. These samples will become invaluable reference tools for future projects.

Good lighting is essential when painting. Evaluate your needs and choose the light best for your space. I recommend Ott-Lites with True Color bulbs. They do not heat the work area and provide excellent lighting.

Water should be easily accessible to your work area, whether it's the kitchen sink or the bathroom. Clean water is essential when painting, so refill your water container often.

PREPARING TO PAINT

Cover your work surface with plastic before starting to set up your supplies and paint. Also cover carpet with plastic or old newspaper to protect it. It is optional to place sandwich paper under the piece being painted. I place sandwich paper under all of my projects. Have two large water containers, one for cleaning brushes and sponges and one for cleaning rubber stamps. The containers should be deep enough so they will not tip but not so deep that they are cumbersome and difficult to use. I prefer Brush Basins by Plaid because they have holes for the brushes and a scrubber on the bottom of the container.

A sample featuring rubber stamping, dry sponging, permanent-marker lines, and applicator-tipped highlights.

Keep a large stack of paper towels beside the water containers. Fold paper towels in half before starting to paint. The towels will take less space and are also more absorbent when doubled. Place a stack of palette paper beside the paper towels. Have a scrub brush handy to clean rubber stamps and dirty fingers.

Wear an old shirt, apron, artist's smock, or comfortable old clothing. It is inevitable that you will get paint on you at some point.

Arrange your paint and tools so they are easy to reach. Arrange your paint by color grouping. Put a drop of paint on the lids of the paint jars and bottles for easy identification. Keep your work area organized by placing similar tools beside each other on the work surface.

CLEANING UP

WHEN YOUR CREATIVE endeavors are finished for the day, straighten the work area. It will make it easier to return and start again. Empty the dirty water containers, fold more paper towels, and clean all tools. If you are painting in a nonpermanent space and have to put the supplies away, clean the supplies and put them away for storage.

A doll necklace featuring additional stuffed, stamped, and painted elements.

STORING PAINTED PIECES

HEAT-SET ALL of the painted fabric samples and store them in resealable plastic bags by either color or technique. Store paper samples in the same way. It will make it easier to find them for use in future creative projects. Store them flat so they do not wrinkle.

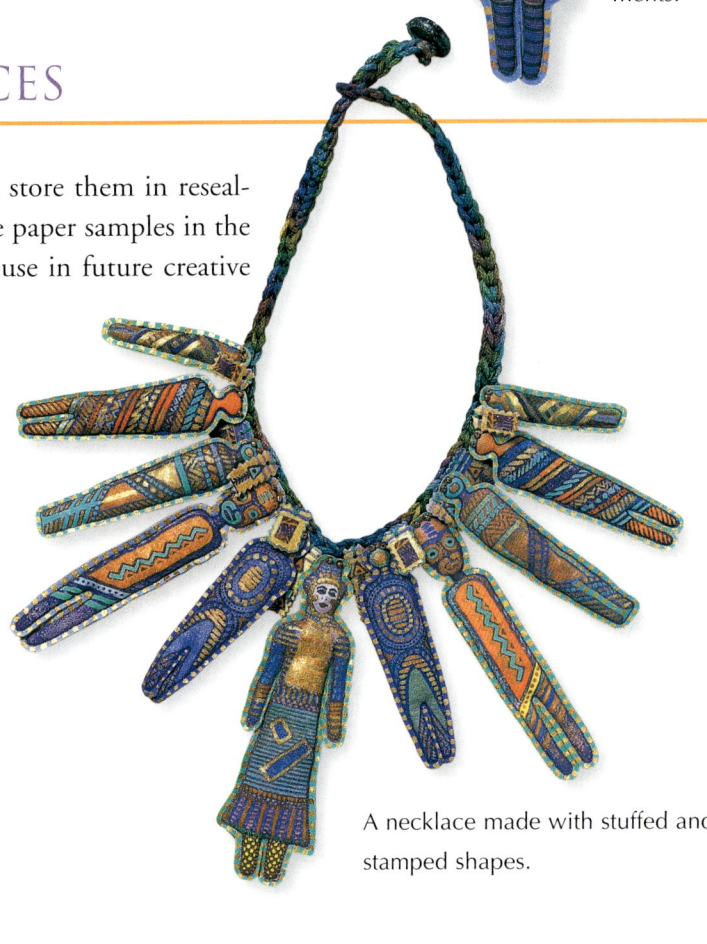

A necklace made with stuffed and stamped shapes.

GETTING STARTED

SPONGE PAINTING

Imagine a **magical** painting tool that costs very little and yet allows you to create **beautiful** textures and **simple** paint washes. The youngest child can hold it. It stores easily and weighs practically nothing. This **magical** tool is a sponge. Different **sponges** give different results.

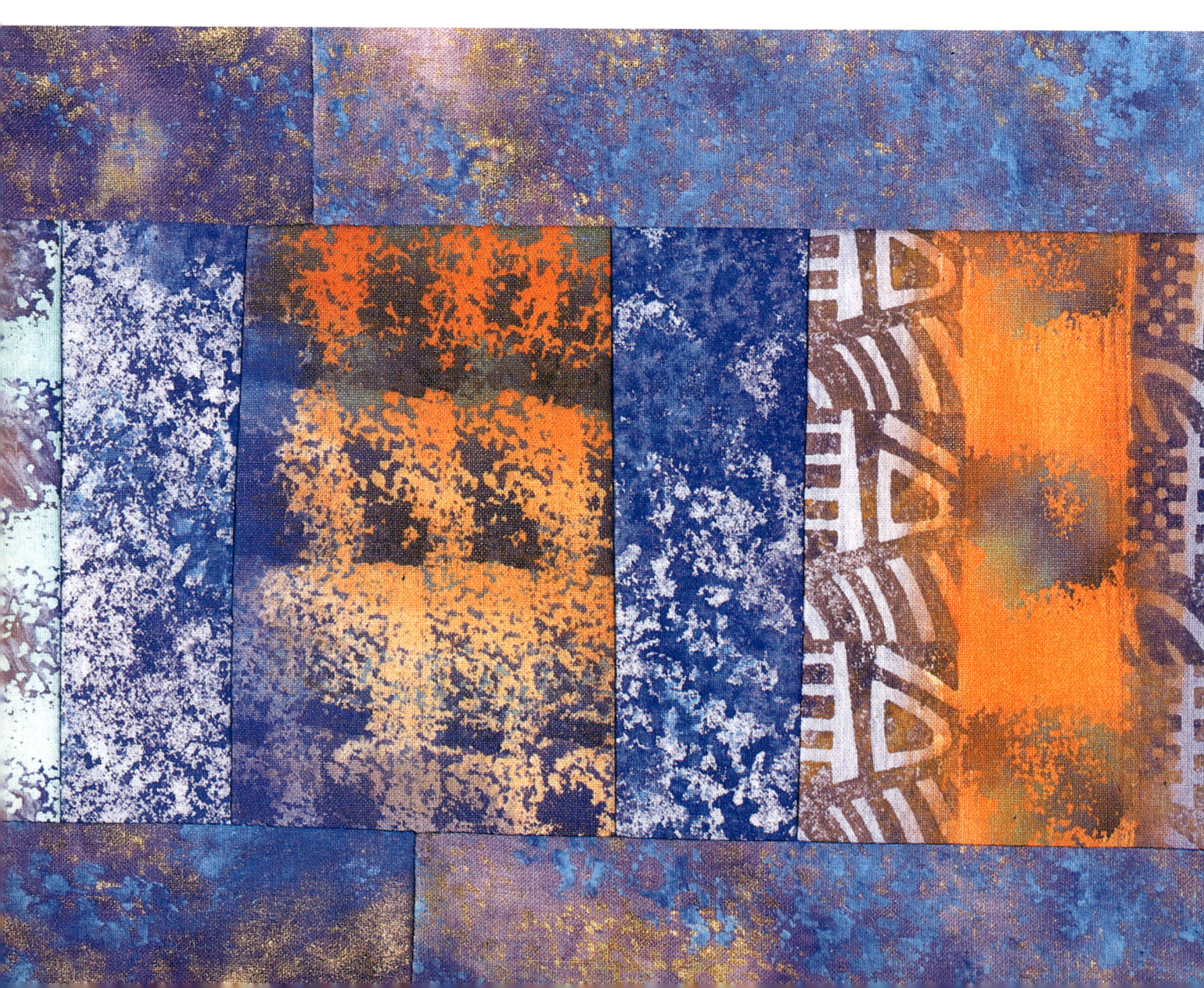

To create bubble patterns on a surface, use sponges with lots of holes. For smooth areas, try less-textured sponges. Pop-up sponges (see "Pop-Up Sponges" on page 26) and sponges that never harden are preferable for applying paint to rubber stamps (see "Rubber Stamping" on page 36). Pop-up sponges are also ideal for applying paint for wet-into-wet effects (see "Wet into Wet" on page 30). Using sponges to apply paint gives quick and beautiful results with very little effort or expense. If sponging fabric paint on fabric, heat-set the finished piece, following the directions on page 14.

BASIC SPONGING

Sponging can be done on practically any surface, with any paint or ink. It is important to use a sponge that never hardens (see "Sponges" on page 18).

Materials

Note: *Refer to the "Getting Started" section on pages 10–21 for information about painting surfaces, paints and coloring agents, tools, and other important information.*

- Paint or ink
- Paint palette
- Sponges
- Paper towels
- Paint surface
- Water container

Instructions

1. Apply one or more paint colors to a palette. If using more than one color, apply the colors to the palette by placing them on top of one another for richer color effects.

Step 3

2. Dip a dry sponge into the wet paint, covering the bottom surface of the sponge; pat the sponge onto a paper towel to remove the excess paint.

3. Sponge the paint onto the paint surface. Repeat the process until you achieve the effect you desire. Varying the pressure applied to the sponge will give different results to the painted piece.

Experiments to Try with Sponging

- Sponge directly onto the paint surface without patting the excess paint onto a paper towel.
- Add more colors to the original palette, and sponge the additional colors onto the creation.
- Sponge onto colored backgrounds.
- Sponge onto a wet surface, or wet your sponge before dipping it into the paint.
- Sponge onto rough and smooth surfaces.

DRY SPONGING

The center panel of this painted sample was first sponged with deep violet paint. After the paint dried, the piece was dry sponged with red-orange paint. The borders are wet-into-wet fabric pieces.

DRY SPONGING IS a very easy and beautiful technique. It produces dramatic effects when paint is sponged onto previously painted, sponged, or rubber-stamped areas (see "Rubber Stamping" on page 36). The color will remain transparent, allowing you to see the paint beneath. This technique works equally well with tape resists (see "Tape Resists" on page 58).

24 SPONGE PAINTING

Materials

- Materials for "Basic Sponging" on page 23

Instructions

1. Dip a dry sponge into a *single* paint color and rub most of the paint onto a paper towel.
2. Sponge paint over the project surface, allowing any previously painted or stamped design to show through.

Step 2

SPONGING REPEAT PATTERNS

This sample has three different examples of repeat patterns with sponges. The background of the large middle panel was created with washes of ivory, red-orange, and violet. The repeated sponged patterns are multicolored, with terra cotta, violet, and light blue. The blue strip near the top was done on a violet painted fabric surface. The sponged repeats are turquoise and violet. The border around the entire piece was done on a multicolored sponged piece, with violet and periwinkle sponged repeat patterns.

REPEAT PATTERNS CAN be printed using sponges of any shape. Simply cut the sponge into the desired shape. You can sponge onto a blank painting surface or one that has been painted. Sponging repeat patterns onto a black surface is especially dramatic.

SPONGE PAINTING 25

Step 3

Materials

- Materials for "Basic Sponging" on page 23
- Kitchen shears or sharp scissors

Instructions

1. Use kitchen shears or sharp scissors to cut out simple shapes from a sponge.

2. Squeeze one or more colors onto the palette and dip the sponge into the paint.

3. Place the painted side of the sponge straight down onto the painting surface, applying even pressure. Lift sponge and repeat. Reapply paint to the sponge as necessary.

POP-UP SPONGES

The main pop-up sponge figure on this piece is a dog that was stamped in violet, red-orange, and terra cotta. A light blue wash was applied with a flat brush near the bottom of the lower row of dogs. An additional sponge was cut into a scallop shape and sponged in a light blue repeat below the lower row of dogs. A wash of red-orange was applied to the upper dogs and most of the lower dogs. The top and bottom borders were created with a pop-up sponge cut into the shape of an elongated horse. The horse designs were sponged onto violet-washed fabric strips. The side borders are wet-into-wet pieces.

POP-UP SPONGES are thin, flat, and firm, and can easily be cut into various shapes with a sharp pair of scissors. Because the sponges start out flat, you can cut intricate designs with a craft knife and a self-healing cutting mat. But remember that children should not be allowed to use sharp cutting tools and must be supervised if doing this project.

When placed in water, pop-up sponges expand to about ½" thick. Wring out the sponges before using them.

Use a pop-up sponge the same way you would a rubber stamp (see "Rubber Stamping" on page 36). You can print with both sides of the sponge to make a mirror image on the paint surface.

Materials

- Materials for "Basic Sponging" on page 23
- Pop-up sponge
- Permanent marker
- Sharp scissors or craft knife and self-healing cutting mat
- Pencil and paper

Instructions

1. Draw your design on a piece of paper with a pencil; cut out the design. Trace the design onto a pop-up sponge with a permanent marker. Cut out the design, using a sharp scissors or a craft knife and a self-healing cutting mat.
2. Place the sponge in the container of water. Wring out the sponge so it is damp, and not soaking wet.
3. Squeeze paint colors onto a palette. Use a small sponge to apply paint to one side of the pop-up sponge, or dip the pop-up sponge into paint on the palette.
4. Print the design onto your painting surface. Repeat as desired.

Step 1

Step 4

SPONGE PAINTING

SPONGING OVER MESH

Previously painted fabric was decorated by applying paint through mesh grids or sequin waste (the strip of plastic remaining after sequins have been punched from it) with a relatively dry sponge. Different grid-painted fabrics can be combined for a multi-textured effect.

Grids and materials with openings can be found in your local craft store in the needlepoint materials area, or look for suitable objects at lumber and hardware stores. I like using sequin waste for this technique. Apply paint with a sponge or toothbrush, which works especially well through small openings. Experiment with different grids and paint and keep a record of the results.

Materials

- Materials for "Basic Sponging" on page 23
- Sequin waste or grid
- Old toothbrush (optional)

Instructions

1. Lay the grid on your painting surface. Apply paint to the palette. Dip a sponge or old toothbrush into the paint. Pat the excess paint onto a paper towel.

2. Apply the paint through the grid openings with the sponge or toothbrush.

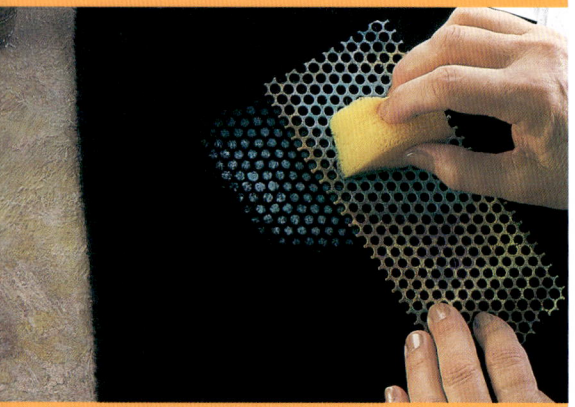

Step 2

WASHES

Washes are easy to create and are used repeatedly for the techniques shown in this book. Washes are nothing more than paint plus water. They can be applied over previously sponged textural areas, over dry rubber-stamped areas (see "Rubber Stamping" on page 36), or any other place where a diluted area of color is needed. If painting a large area with a wash, mix the paint in a small, flat dish. The more water you add, the lighter the wash. When creating washes on fabric, I prefer Dr. Ph. Martin's ReadyTex paints. Pebeo's Setasilk and Jacquard Dye-na-Flow are also wonderful for washes on fabric. Although I usually use sponges, you may also use brushes to apply washes.

This sample combines rubber stamping, crayon rubbings, and brush-painted details. The paint surface was washed with red-orange and yellow-orange paint.

Materials

- Materials for "Basic Sponging" on page 23
- Small, flat disposable containers or dishes
- Eyedropper
- Flat paintbrush (optional)

Instructions

1. Place a small amount of paint in a disposable container; use a different container for each color of paint. Dilute the paint by adding drops of water with an eyedropper.

2. Use a damp or wet sponge or brush to apply paint to the project surface. Reapply layers of paint as desired; layers of washes give beautiful results.

Step 2

SPONGE PAINTING 29

Freezer-Paper Protection

Washes and wet-into-wet pieces (see "Wet into Wet" on page 30) can be very messy. It is important to place the piece to be painted on a waterproof surface. Use pieces of freezer paper larger than the painted piece to protect your work surface. Place the work on the freezer paper and apply the paint. The freezer paper can then be set in another area to dry, leaving your work surface free for other projects.

WET INTO WET

After the surface of the paper was sprayed with water, different paint colors were applied with a brush, allowing the colors to bleed together. The finished design was mounted on two pieces of coordinating paper to create a framed border around the artwork.

WET-INTO-WET techniques involve using very wet paint on a very wet surface. The paint spreads and interacts, creating beautiful patterns. Inks, water-colors, diluted acrylics, and diluted fabric paint can be used when

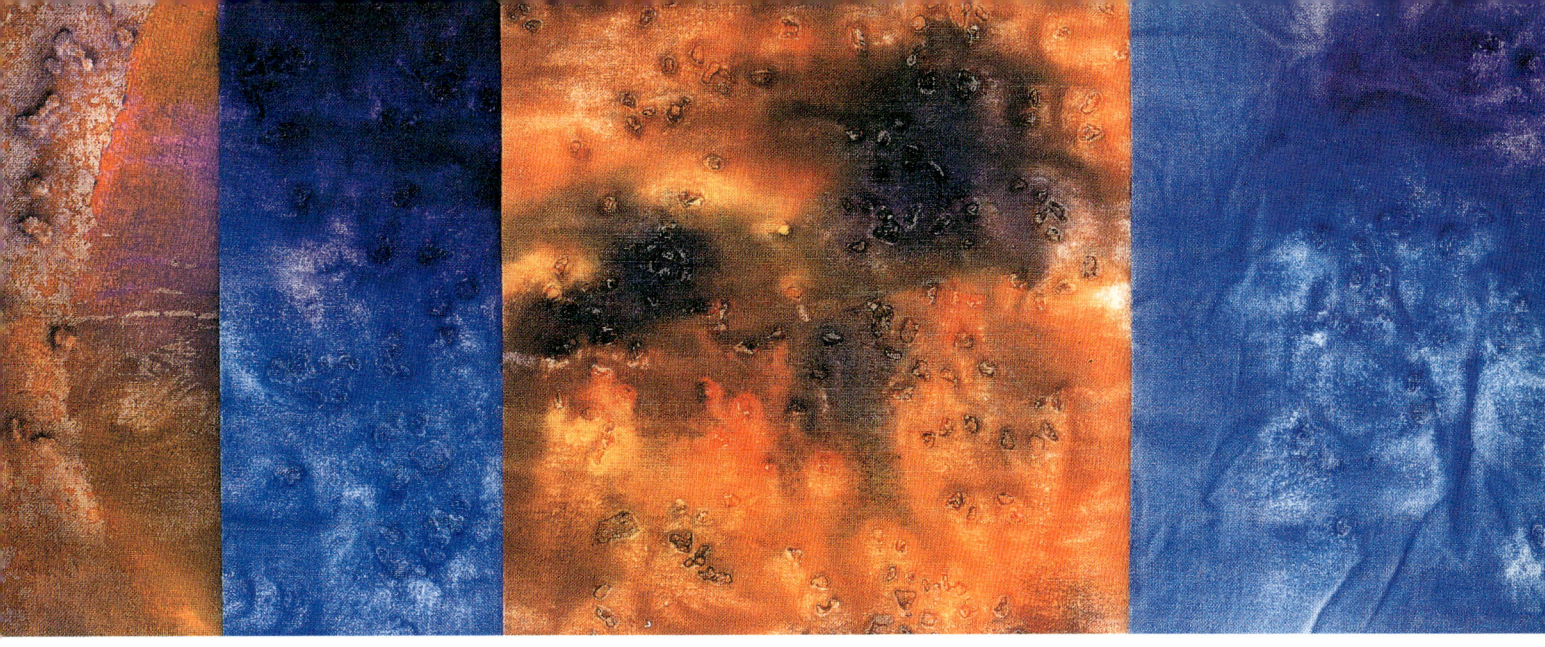

creating wet-into-wet pieces. Acrylic paints become stiff on fabric, and inks and watercolors wash out of fabric. When choosing paint for your creative project, read the manufacturer's suggestions. Experiment with different paints, inks, dyes, and acrylics and keep a record of your findings. For wet-into-wet applications on fabric, I prefer Dr. Ph. Martin's ReadyTex fabric paint because of its color intensity.

Materials

- Materials for "Basic Sponging" on page 23
- Small, flat dishes or small disposable cups
- Eyedropper
- Spray bottle (optional)
- Flat paintbrushes (optional)

Instructions

1. Spray water on the paint surface, using a spray bottle, or dip fabric or lightweight paper into clean water and wring it out slightly.
2. Place a small amount of paint in a cup or flat dish. Dilute paint with a water-filled eyedropper. More water will result in a lighter color. Less water will result in a darker color. Use a separate cup or dish for each paint color.
3. Apply the paint to the wet surface, using a damp or wet sponge or brush.

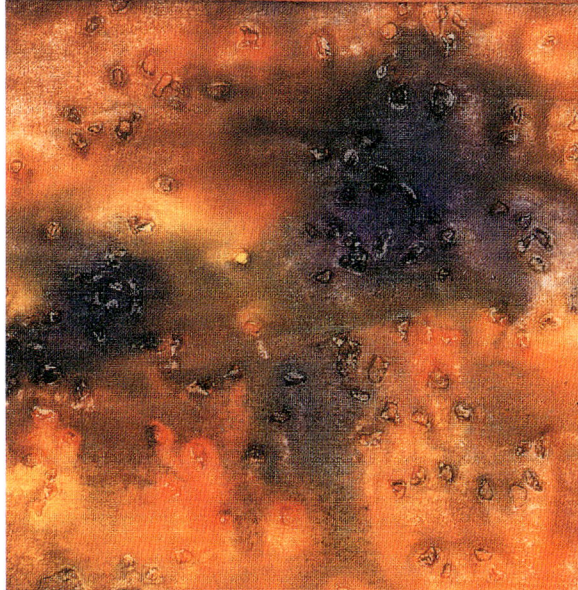

Step 3

SCRUNCHED WET INTO WET

Violet, aqua, blue, and turquoise paints were used in the left and right scrunched borders. Violet, burnt sienna, and yellow ochre paints were used in the center panel. The bottom border was done with a wet-into-wet technique using salt. Violet, yellow ochre, orange, and aqua paints were used on the bottom border.

By scrunching wet fabric or lightweight paper into a small container, you can create spectacular pieces for creative projects. Use a container with a lid or place the container in a resealable plastic bag. The container is important since it confines the piece, creating the wonderful paint textures. Placing the piece loosely in a bag will not create the same effect. If you leave the piece overnight, the result will be very dramatic. If you cannot leave it contained overnight, try to leave it for at least two to three hours.

Use scrunched fabric pieces in quilts, tear the fabric into strips to make fabric ribbons, or use the fabric in other creative projects. Scrunched papers can be used for journals or greeting cards.

Materials

- Materials for "Basic Sponging" on page 23 (paint surface should be fabric or lightweight paper)
- Small, disposable cups or flat dishes
- Eyedropper
- Resealable plastic bag or small plastic container with lid

Instructions

1. Dip a piece of fabric or lightweight paper into water, wring it out slightly, and lay it flat on your work surface.

2. Dilute a small amount of paint in a disposable cup, using a water-filled eyedropper. Use a separate cup for each color of paint. Apply slightly diluted paint colors to the fabric or paper, using a separate sponge for each color. An eyedropper may also be used to apply color to the wrinkled surface.

3. Crumple the piece into a ball, place it in a small container, and cover with a lid. Or place the container in a resealable plastic bag. Allow to dry for at least 2 to 3 hours or overnight.

4. Remove the piece from the container and let it dry completely on a waterproof surface. For fabric projects, thoroughly spray the dried painting with water and heat-set, following the manufacturer's directions.

Step 3

SALT TEXTURES

A salt-textured piece created with varying degrees of violet, red-orange, and yellow-orange paint. Rock salt was added to the wet paint to create the texture.

FOR ADDED TEXTURE in your painted designs, drop salt onto wet-into-wet creations. The salt creates starburst effects or it leaves darker patterns on the painted surface. Different salts give different effects. I prefer rock salt, but experimenting with different salts will give you

Step 3

valuable information when you're choosing a salt for a particular project. The paint must be very wet for this process to work. Both the surface being painted and the type of paint used affect the results. Darker paint colors give more dramatic results.

Materials

- Materials for "Basic Sponging" on page 23
- Rock salt
- Spray bottle

Instructions

1. Spray water onto the paint surface.
2. Apply wet paint to the surface with a damp or wet sponge. If using tube or jar paint, you must dilute the paint. If using inks, dyes, or Dr. Ph. Martin's ReadyTex, the paint is ready to use and no dilution is needed.
3. Sprinkle salt onto the wet paint.
4. Let the paint dry; then remove the salt by brushing it off with your fingers.

PLASTIC WRAP PATTERNS

Plastic wrap on wet paint creates an incredible effect. This technique was created by Maxine Masterfield. It can be done on any surface where wet-into-wet techniques can be used. A variation of this technique is to use waxed paper instead of plastic wrap. It is also possible to lay pieces of paper toweling or tissue paper on wet paint to create patterns. Laying absorbent materials on the wet paint will result in the paint being lighter wherever the absorbent materials touch the paint surface. Some artists place wet pieces in a freezer to create ice crystals in the paint. The results will vary each time you do this process, and the paint must be very wet for this technique to work. Contrasting paint colors also create more dramatic pieces. Try different paint surfaces and different paint, and keep a record of the results.

Materials

- Materials for "Basic Sponging" on page 23
- Plastic wrap

Instructions

1. Wet the paint surface with a sponge, and apply different paint colors to the wet surface with sponges. Intense colors work best.

2. Lay a piece of plastic wrap onto the piece. Manipulate the plastic wrap into hills and valleys. Some parts will touch the paint surface and others will not. Wherever the plastic wrap touches the wet paint, the color will be darker. The ridges that do not touch the wet paint will be lighter.

3. Let the piece dry, then remove the plastic wrap.

Step 2

Yellow-orange, red-orange, light blue, and violet paint were applied to a wet surface with a sponge. A piece of plastic wrap was laid on the piece, and the hills and valleys of the plastic wrap were manipulated to create the veinlike texture.

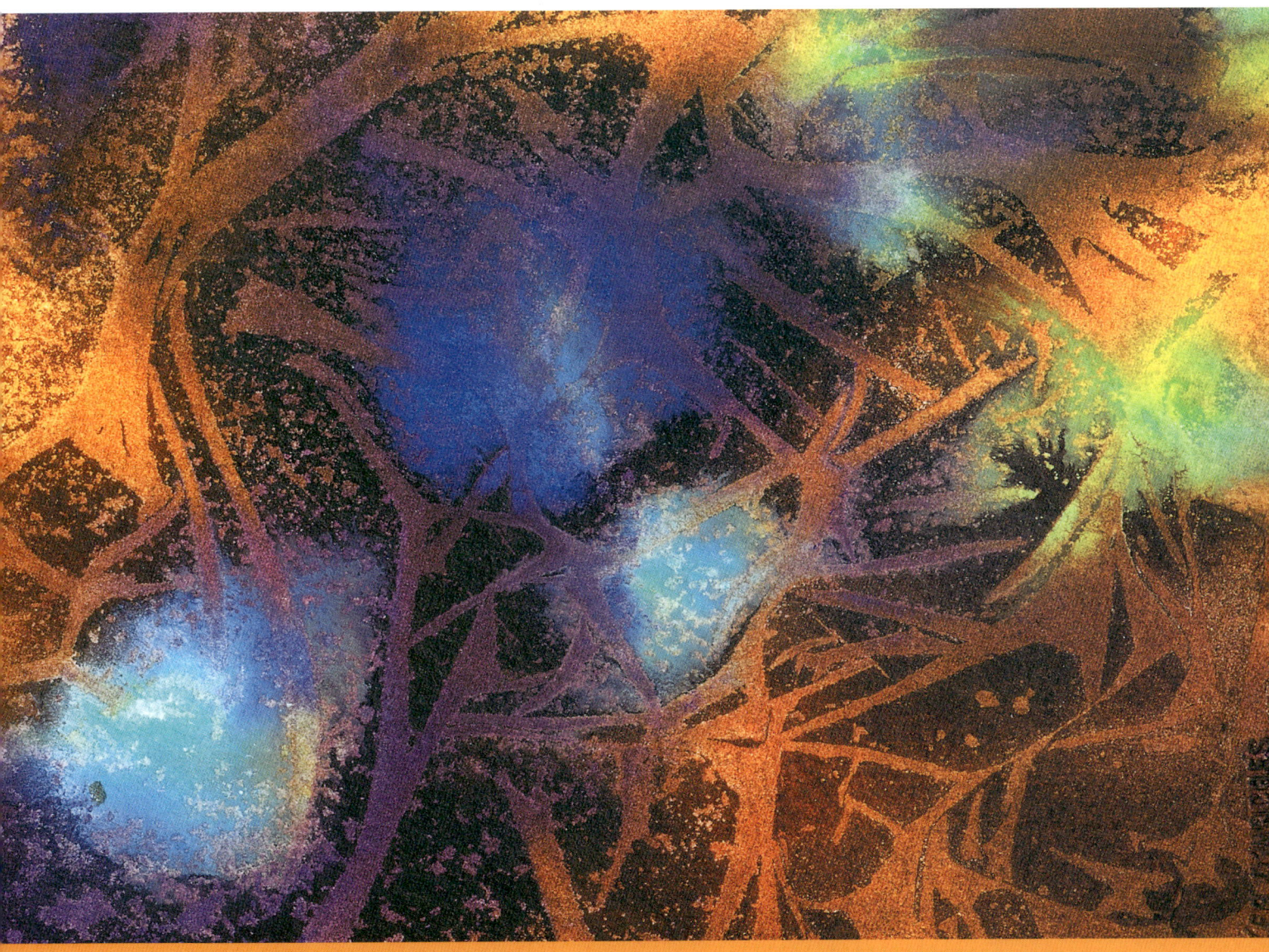

SPONGE PAINTING 35

RUBBER STAMPING

I started **collecting** rubber stamps more than twenty years ago when a **teacher** in the language department of my high school **shared** his collection with me. The only rubber stamps available then were clip art, but they opened a **magical** world for my students and me, and I collected them **avidly**

FOUR AND A HALF years ago, my husband, Joel, and I decided that we would create our own small rubber stamp company. The images used throughout the book are from our company, Impress Me. Our stamps are deeply etched and unmounted, allowing for a wide range of uses and applications. The stamps are thick enough to use without mounting. Unmounted rubber stamps offer the flexibility of working on curved or unusual surfaces. Repeat patterns are also easily produced, and it is easy to see where the stamp is being placed onto the surface when the stamp is unmounted. Since I use a variety of paints, the ease of cleaning is another advantage when working with these stamps. Dirty stamps can be submerged in water, then cleaned with a toothbrush and water.

When using paint on your stamps, be careful to clean them immediately after use with a brush and water. Do not submerge mounted rubber stamps in water since the glues used to mount them could weaken. If you're using Impress Me stamps, however, you can safely leave them submerged in water to soak.

To clean off stamp-pad ink, a dampened washcloth or a tray with moistened paper towels works well. Some stamp artists use a mixture of one part window-cleaning liquid with one part water to clean stamp-pad ink off rubber stamps. Place the cleaning mixture on a paper towel or old washcloth, then rub the stamp over the wet surface.

Rubber stamps are invaluable tools in producing creative artwork, and they can be used in many ways. They can be used with other art media, enhancing the final creative piece. Experiment with rubber stamps. You will be amazed at the possibilities.

RUBBER STAMPING WITH PAINT

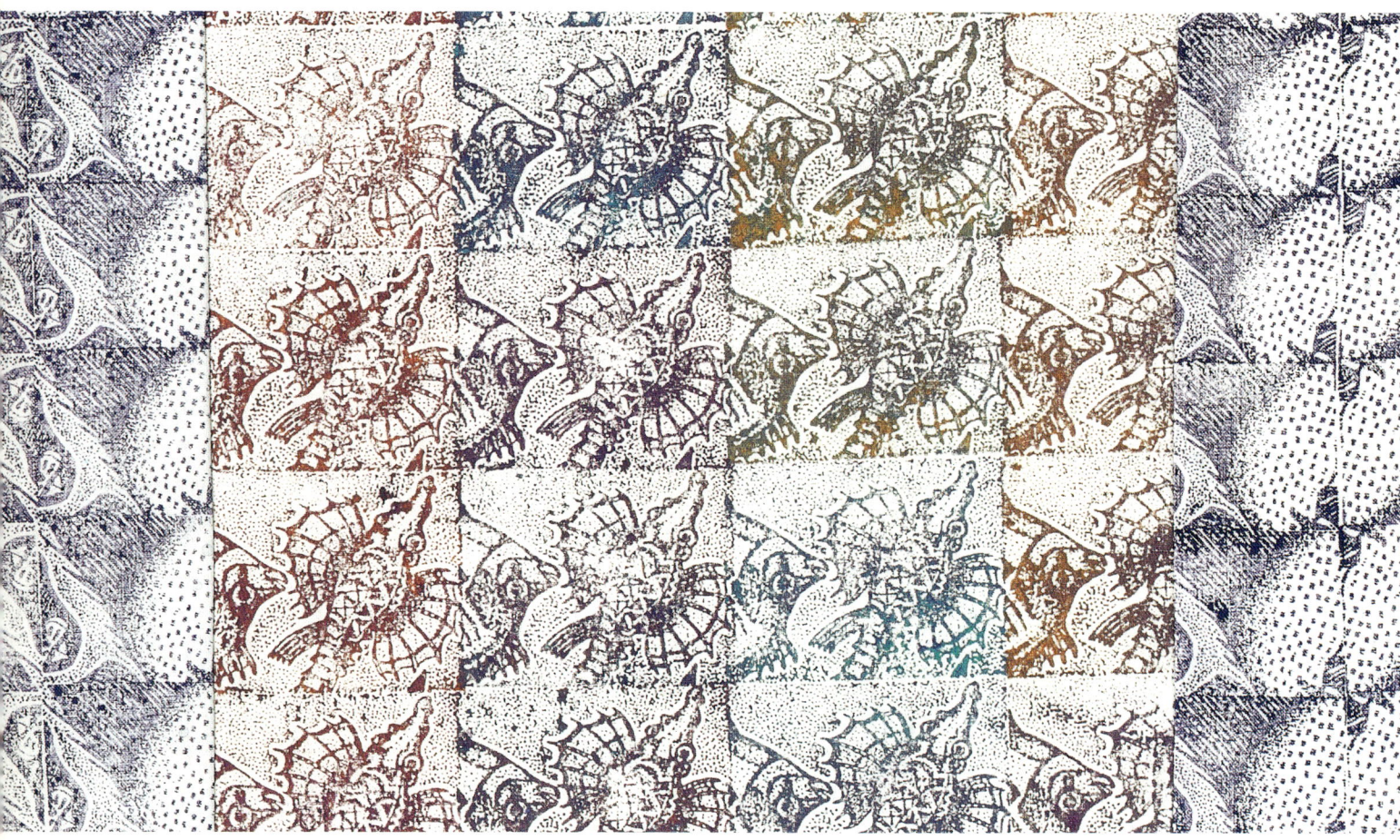

The middle section of the sample was done with one stamp. Violet, terra cotta, and burgundy acrylic paints were squeezed on top of one another on the paint palette, then sponged onto the rubber stamp. The sides were done with violet fabric paint from a stamp pad.

RUBBER STAMPING WITH paint is completely different than rubber stamping with stamp pads. More than one color in the paint mix gives exciting results. It's possible to make excellent impressions with acrylic paint. You can use tube, jar, or bottled acrylics. If the paint is too thick, use an eyedropper to add water to the paint mix and stir together with a flat brush or stir stick before rubber stamping. Apply the paint to the rubber stamp with a small, *dry* sponge.

Fabric paint works like acrylic paints when rubber stamping on fabric. Thin fabric paint will not work well. Use jar or thick bottled fabric paint when rubber stamping. Most fabric paints have textile extenders for thinning the paint, although I prefer using water to dilute the paint. Experiment to see which products work best for the project you are doing.

Dark surfaces are especially dramatic for rubber stamping and look best when painted with lighter-color paints. Metallic and pearlescent colors are beautiful when stamped on a contrasting surface.

Materials

NOTE: *Refer to the "Getting Started" section on pages 10–21 for information about painting surfaces, paints and coloring agents, tools, and other important subjects.*

- Paint
- Paint palette, if using paint
- Rubber stamps
- Paper towels
- Dry sponge squares, if using paint
- Paint surface
- Old toothbrush
- Water container, if using paint

Step 1

Instructions

1. Squeeze one or more colors on top of one another on the palette. Place the rubber stamp face up on a paper towel. Dip a dry sponge square into the paint and apply the paint evenly onto the stamp, making sure to cover the surface completely.

2. Turn the stamp facedown onto the project and apply even pressure to the back of the stamp with your fingers.

3. Remove the stamp from the surface. Repeat the stamping process as desired.

4. Clean the stamp with a toothbrush and water immediately after use, unless using unmounted stamps, which you can place in water to soak for a while.

Step 2

Step 3

RUBBER STAMPING

RUBBER STAMPING WITH INK PADS

This piece was stamped with a rubber stamp pad, and washes were applied.

Rubber stamp pads are the most popular form of getting color onto rubber stamps. It's possible to achieve incredible detail when using rubber stamp pads.

Materials

- Materials for "Rubber Stamping with Paint" on page 38 (use stamp-pad ink instead of paint)

Instructions

1. Pat the stamp pad onto the rubber stamp, covering the stamp completely with ink.

2. Press the stamp facedown onto the desired surface. Remove the stamp and repeat as desired.

3. Clean the stamp immediately when finished, using a damp cloth or paper towels.

Rubber-Stamped Ribbons

You can customize ribbons with painted designs just as easily as you can stamp designs on fabric. There are a variety of ribbon types, colors, and widths available from floral-supply houses, craft stores, and fabric stores, and all will rubber stamp beautifully. Unmounted stamps work great for repeat patterns. Follow the directions for "Rubber Stamping with Paint" or "Rubber Stamping with Ink Pads." Remember to heat-set fabric paints.

If desired, apply a wash over the stamped ribbon for added color.

Repeat Patterns and Borders with Rubber Stamps

Doing repeat patterns—on borders, for example—is simple with unmounted, deeply etched rubber stamps. Stamp the images side by side until satisfied with the results. Leave the piece as is or apply a wash over it.

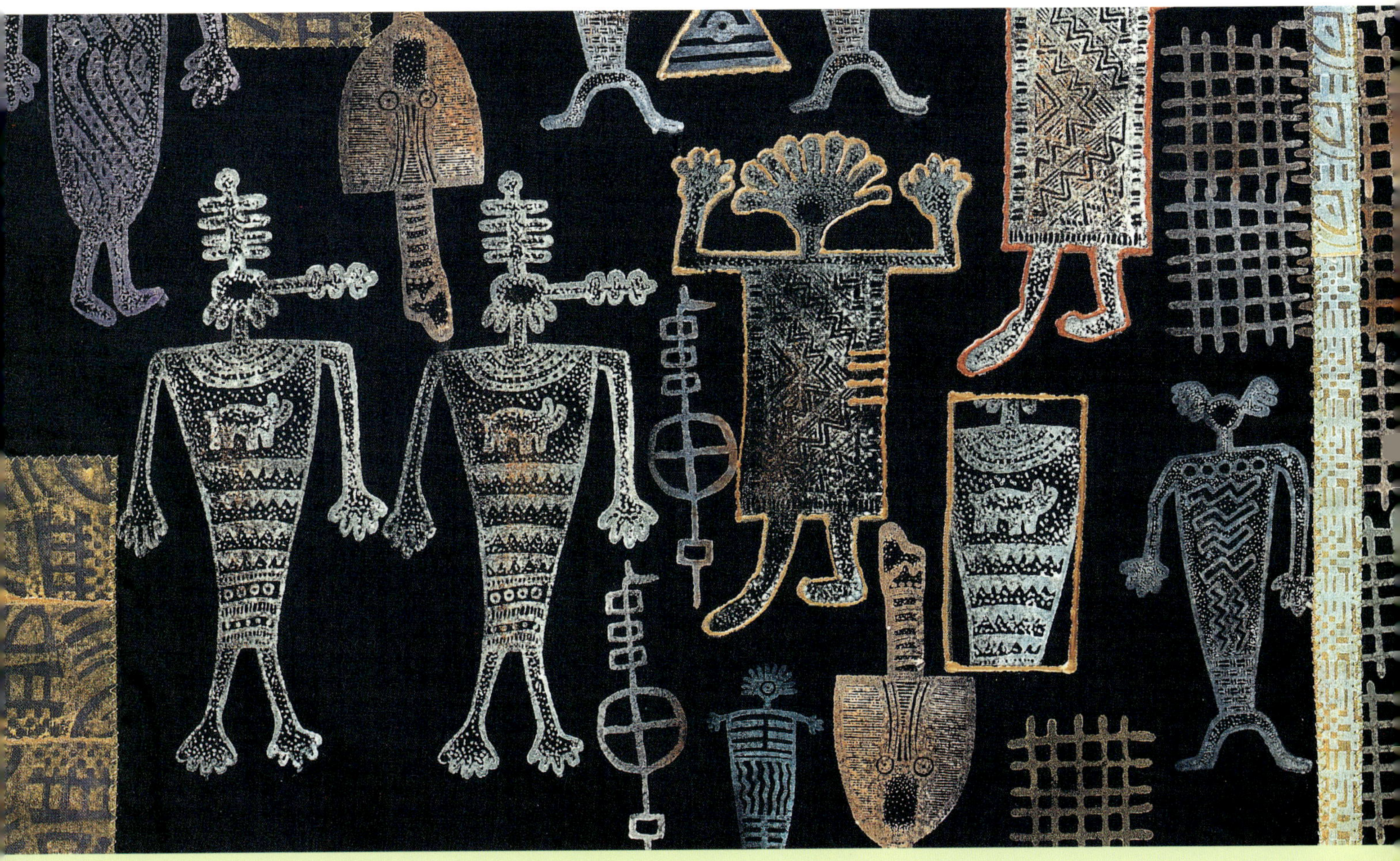

TECHNIQUES FOR ALTERNATIVE TOOLS

There are many ways to apply **color** to your surface without using traditional tools. Look around the house. Almost **every** room will yield **possible** tools for applying paint or color. This section covers using applicator-tipped paint, markers, old credit cards, toothbrushes, plastic utensils, cardboard, painting combs, and brayers. These are only some of the **wonderful** items that you can use.

APPLICATOR-TIPPED PAINT TECHNIQUES

APPLICATOR-TIPPED PAINT comes in many forms. I recommend Tulip by Duncan, Jones Tones, and Plaid brands for wonderful results. Before using the paint, shake it well to dissipate any bubbles that might be in the bottle. Test the paint on a paper towel before applying it to the paint surface. Use applicator-tipped paint to outline finished stamped and painted areas or to draw lines and dots for textural interest. After the paint dries, leave it as is, or apply washes (see "Washes" on page 29) over the dry paint.

Materials

NOTE: *Refer to the "Getting Started" section on pages 10–21 for information about painting surfaces, paints and coloring agents, tools, and other important subjects.*

- Paint surface
- Applicator-tipped paint
- Paint palette
- Paper towels
- Water container
- Old credit card
- Plastic knife, fork, or old comb

Lines, dots, and scrapings in different colors of applicator-tipped paint were used to create the left strip of this art piece. Multicolored washes were applied over the dried paint. The wide middle strip also features lines and dots, with one scraping in a single color of applicator-tipped paint and one scraping in multicolored applicator-tipped paint. The whole strip has five different paint washes applied in stripes. On the wide right hand strip, a variety of scraped applicator-tipped paints was applied. A violet wash was applied after the paint dried.

Experiment: Applicator-tip painting

Experiment: Credit card scraping

Experiment: Plastic knife scraping

Experiment: Outlining with applicator-tipped paint

Experiments to Try with Applicator-Tipped Paints

- Gently squeeze the applicator-tipped bottle and practice drawing lines, zigzags, swirls, dashes, patterns, dots, and any other pattern that comes to mind. Practice is essential when using applicator-tipped paints. It's easier to make short, continuous lines than a single very long line. Move your hand back and forth in short, overlapping strokes as you apply the paint.

- Apply one or more colors in a line, applying colors on top of each other. Scrape the colors with an old driver's license or credit card and pull the paint down the paint surface (see "Scraping Paint with a Credit Card" on page 47).

- Apply one or more colors in a line. Use a plastic knife, fork, or old comb to pull the paint down the paint surface. The knife, fork, or comb you use will affect the results. Experiment with similar tools.

- Use applicator-tipped paint to outline previously painted areas.

44   TECHNIQUES FOR ALTERNATIVE TOOLS

Heat-Setting Tips

When using applicator-tipped paint on fabric, you don't need to heat-set it; it will go through repeated washings without coming off the fabric. Applicator-tipped paint can be applied after heat-setting fabric paint on fabric. If you apply the applicator-tipped paint before heat-setting the fabric, be sure to cover the fabric with sandwich or parchment paper to protect the iron from the paint.

INK BLEED WITH MARKERS

A combination of permanent and washable markers, gel rollers, and ballpoint pens were used in this sample. The colored lines were sprayed with water to create exciting bleeds of color.

TECHNIQUES FOR ALTERNATIVE TOOLS

AN ENORMOUS VARIETY of markers, colored ballpoint pens, and gel rollers are available at any office or art-supply store. Some are washable and some are permanent. I have a large collection of these tools, and it's fun to combine them into one composition and then spray the entire piece with water. The nonpermanent inks bleed to make free-form patterns on the paint surface. Blotting the ink with paper towels or fabric stops the process. You can further enhance your projects with other paint techniques if desired. Explore metallic markers, since many add permanent, exciting detail to finished projects.

You can also purchase markers made for fabric. Follow the manufacturer's instructions when using these markers. They must be heat-set before washing.

Step 1

Materials

NOTE: *Refer to the "Getting Started" section on pages 10–21 for information about painting surfaces, paints and coloring agents, tools, and other important subjects.*

- Paint surface
- Washable and permanent markers
- Gel rollers
- Colored ballpoint pens
- Spray bottle
- Paper towels or fabric scraps

Instructions

1. Draw a design onto a paint surface, using a variety of markers, gel rollers, and ballpoint pens.
2. Using a spray bottle, wet the design with water, allowing some of the drawn lines to bleed.
3. Blot the wet design with paper towels or fabric scraps. Repeat the process if desired.

Experiments to Try with Markers, Gel Rollers, and Ballpoint Pens

- Use permanent markers to add line and texture to an existing creative project.
- Use permanent markers to color in rubber-stamped or painted areas.
- Use permanent markers to highlight areas difficult to paint with a brush.
- Use permanent markers to write words on a project.

Step 2

CREDIT CARD TECHNIQUES

CREDIT CARDS ARE magical painting tools. You can use them to apply paint to any surface, or to print lines and edges. You can cut them into different sizes for more creative possibilities, or cut notches in them to create textural areas when applying paint. Because credit cards are stiff, scraping is quite easy and fun to do. Layers of scraped paint result in gorgeous painted surfaces. Different paint will yield different results. Transparent and opaque paints can be combined for interesting effects. Combine the credit card process with other painting techniques to produce exciting painted surfaces.

Layers of color, scraped with a credit card, were used to create this sample. Lines were added to the composition by printing the edge of the credit card. Different sizes of credit cards were used to paint smaller and larger areas.

Scraping Paint with a Credit Card

Materials

NOTE: *Refer to the "Getting Started" section on pages 10–21 for information about painting surfaces, paints and coloring agents, tools, and other important subjects.*

- Old credit cards
- Scissors
- Paint
- Paint palette
- Paint surface
- Paper towels
- Water container

Step 2

Step 1

Instructions

1. Cut a credit card or old driver's license into various widths, or cut notches into the credit card if desired.

2. Squeeze paint onto the surface and pull the paint across the surface with the edge of the credit card. Repeat as desired to build up layers of color.

3. Clean the credit card with a paper towel when finished.

Printing with a Credit Card

Materials

- Materials for "Scraping Paint with a Credit Card" on page 47

Instructions

1. Dip the edge of a credit card into a thin layer of paint on a palette. Press the edge of the credit card onto the paint surface to print the line (you can print the line over a previously painted surface). Widen the line by scraping the paint slightly with the edge of the card.

2. Reapply paint and repeat the process as desired.

TOOTHBRUSH SPATTER

OLD TOOTHBRUSHES ARE wonderful painting tools. Achieve airbrushing effects by spattering layers of colors over a paint surface. Spattered color adds textural interest to any paint creation. The thickness of the paint and how close the toothbrush is to the surface also affect the final result. Experiment with different paint and keep a record for future creations.

Materials

NOTE: *Refer to the "Getting Started" section on pages 10–21 for information about painting surfaces, paints and coloring agents, tools, and other important subjects.*

- Toothbrush
- Paints
- Paint palette
- Paper towels
- Paint surface
- Plastic knife
- Water container

This sample was created by rubber stamping a doll image. A freezer-paper block over the doll was used to add the rubber-stamped wings (see page 61). A rubber-stamped border was added to the bottom of the center panel and to the side of the angel doll. The entire piece was spattered with various paint colors for texture. The top and bottom borders were rubber stamped.

Instructions

1. Dip a toothbrush into slightly diluted paint and pat the excess paint onto a paper towel.
2. Hold a plastic knife in one hand, and run the edge of the toothbrush *away* from you, across the hard edge of the plastic knife. Repeat as desired.

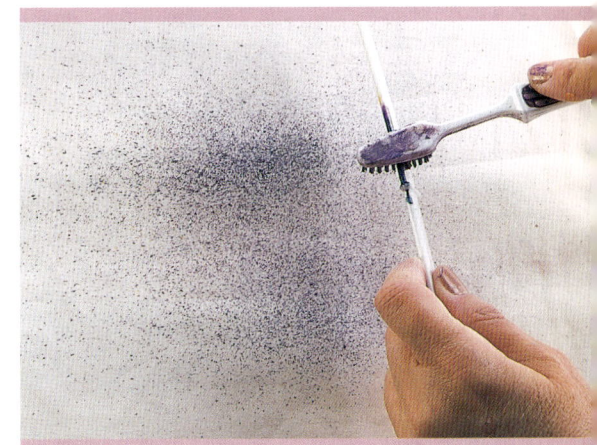

Step 2

TECHNIQUES FOR ALTERNATIVE TOOLS

In this sample, layers of color were applied to a black background with Ranger brayers of various widths. The paint was applied to rough and smooth surfaces. A little rubber stamping completes the project.

BRAYERS

BRAYERS PROVIDE AN easy and fun way to apply paint to a surface. Brayers are available at craft and hobby stores in many shapes, widths, and sizes, and each has its own properties when applying paint. Many large hardware stores also sell brayers. Plaid Enterprises, Inc., manufactures wonderful foam brayers, called Fun to Paint rollers. Fiskars has a line of brayers with interesting patterns and textures. Ranger manufactures brayers that snap out of their holders, making it easy to put rubber bands or string around the brayers to create unusual effects.

Materials

NOTE: *Refer to the "Getting Started" section on pages 10–21 for information about painting surfaces, paints and coloring agents, tools, and other important subjects.*

- Paint
- Paint palette
- Brayers
- Paint surface
- Paper towels
- Plastic tray to hold paint (optional)
- Water container

Experiment: Applying paint with a brayer

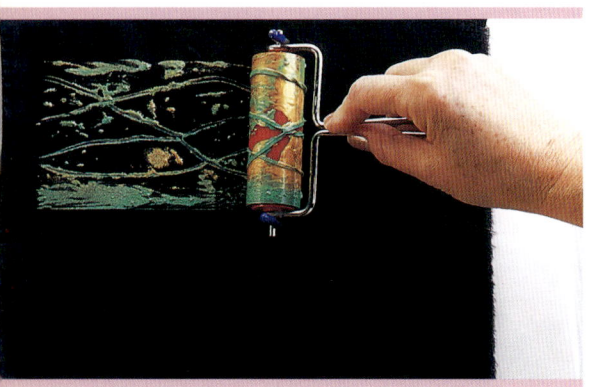

Experiment: Applying paint with a rubber-band wrapped brayer

Experiments to Try with Brayers

- Roll a brayer through one or more colors of paint, and roll the paint onto the surface. Repeat as desired.
- Create an interesting brayer by putting rubber bands or string around a Ranger brayer. Roll the brayer through paint and apply it to the painting surface.

Creating and Painting Textural Surfaces

It's great fun to create textural surfaces with gesso, gels, or acrylic paints. A variation of this technique was first introduced by Virginia Lee Williams and Nita Leland. Their method involved using a brayer to cover heavy tissue paper with gesso to texturize a surface, and then applying paint to the uneven surface with another paint-loaded brayer.

Any surface, including fabric, can be texturized with gesso, gels, or acrylic paint, and you can create spectacular painted papers. I've discovered that sandwich paper, which is much more durable than tissue paper, works beautifully (see "Paper" on page 11). Black gesso or acrylic produces dramatic results. If fabric is used, the finished piece will be very stiff. Apply paint with brayers to the textured surface.

Materials

NOTE: *Refer to the "Getting Started" section on pages 10–21 for information about painting surfaces, paints and coloring agents, tools, and other important subjects.*

- Gesso, white or colored; gel medium; or liquid acrylic paint
- Heavy tissue paper, sandwich paper, or fabric
- Brayers
- Colored paint
- Paint palette
- Paper towels
- Plastic tray to hold paint (optional)
- Water container
- Materials for "Rubber Stamping" on page 36 (optional)

Instructions

1. Apply gesso, gel medium, or acrylic paint to heavy tissue paper, sandwich paper, or fabric with a brayer to create a textured surface. Allow to dry.
2. Apply colored paint to the textured surface with a brayer. Enhance the piece with rubber stamping if desired (see "Rubber Stamping" on page 36).

This sample was made on tissue paper, brayered with black gesso from Golden. Paint was then applied with a brayer, and stamping with metallic paint completes the sample.

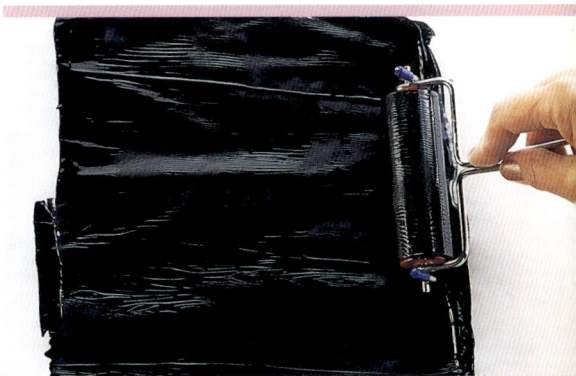

Step 1

This sample was created by painting a single piece of fabric with different scraped painting techniques, small foam-plate prints, and rubber stamping. The fabric was cut into two pieces, and then rejoined with a violet painted band between them for a more interesting finished piece.

TECHNIQUES FOR TEXTURE TOOLS

You can create textured areas by combing through paint mixed with Faux Finish Glaze Base from Delta Technical Coatings, using a variety of scraping tools. Try wall combs from the paint department. Plaid's paint combs can be used to create a variety of textures. Notched plastic tools used to apply mastic for floor tile can also be used for this technique. You can purchase these combs at paint, craft, and hardware stores, or you can create your own tools by cutting notches in old credit cards. Different edges produce different results. Experiment by combining different paints with the Faux Finish Glaze Base. A textured surface will be a little stiff on fabric, but small pieces can be used for appliqué or jewelry. Experiment to discover the possibilities. Scraped painted pieces can be combined with other painting techniques.

Materials

NOTE: *Refer to the "Getting Started" section on pages 10–21 for information about painting surfaces, paints and coloring agents, tools, and other important subjects.*

- Bottled craft acrylic paint
- Paint palette
- Paint surface
- Paper towels
- Delta's Faux Finish Glaze Base
- Large, flat brush
- Paint combs, old credit cards, or multi-use adhesive spreader with notched edges (available at hardware and paint stores)
- Water container

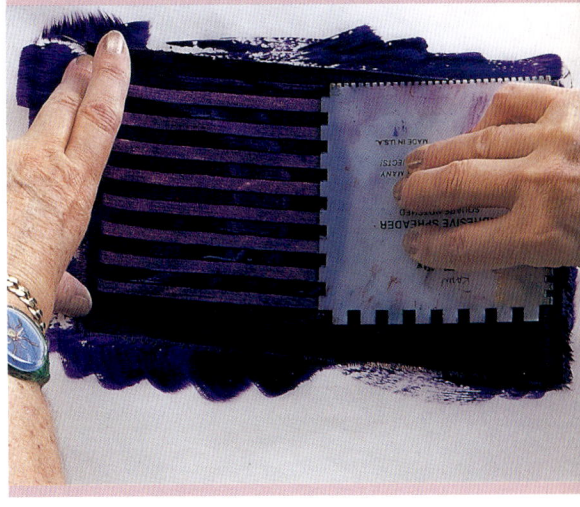

Step 1

Instructions

1. Brush a solid layer of bottled craft acrylic paint onto the paint surface; allow to dry. Mix equal parts of the same bottled acrylic paint and Delta's Faux Finish Glaze Base; brush it onto the surface. While wet, scrape the second layer of paint with a paint comb, old credit card, or multi-use adhesive spreader.

2. Let the second layer dry and reapply color as desired.

TECHNIQUES FOR ALTERNATIVE TOOLS

RESISTS

The word *resist*, when used in conjunction with painting, means **anything** on the painting surface that **resists** being covered by paint. Resists can be tape, pieces of paper, **crayons** or other waxy substances, modeling **paste,** applicator-tipped paint, dried paint, freezer paper, gel medium, or gesso. Experiment to **discover** the **possibilities,** and take notes on each process for future reference.

 List each step in the order that it was completed so that you can repeat it. Each resist technique gives a very different result, and most of these techniques can be used together or in conjunction with the other techniques shown throughout this book.

PAINT RESISTS

Paint becomes a resist once it has dried. Washes (see page 29) can be applied over the dried paint without the paint smearing or running. Acrylic paint makes an excellent resist for future washes. Fabric paint can also act as a resist, even before it's heat-set. The majority of the samples in this book involve applying layers of paint, either by stamping or sponging first (see "Rubber Stamping" on page 36 and "Sponge Painting" on page 22), then applying washes.

CRAYON BATIK

Crayon batik involves applying crayon rubbings on fabric or lightweight paper and then placing washes (see page 55) over the waxy rubbings. Fabric crayon batiks can be appliquéd to cloth or glued to other projects. Crayon batik can be applied directly on T-shirts or items of clothing. The washes will run, so take that into consideration when using this technique.

This sample has three wide panels, each show-ing a unique crayon batik design. Different rubber stamps and different colors were used for each panel.

Step 1

Step 2

Step 3

Materials

NOTE: *Refer to the "Getting Started" section on pages 10–21 for information about painting surfaces, paints and coloring agents, tools, and other important subjects.*

- Rubber stamps, variety of deeply etched and unmounted
- Medium-grit sandpaper
- Piece of fabric or lightweight paper
- Crayons
- Liquid paint
- Disposable plastic cups
- Eyedropper
- Paper towels
- Sponges
- Water container

Instructions

1. Place a number of deeply etched, unmounted rubber stamps face up and side by side on a piece of sandpaper.

2. Lay a piece of fabric or lightweight paper over the rubber stamps. Using the side of a crayon, rub across the rubber stamps; press hard on the crayon so that the impression is very waxy. Change crayon colors as desired.

3. Place liquid paint in a disposable cup, using a separate cup for each color; dilute with water, using an eyedropper. Using a different sponge for each color, apply washes over the waxy impressions, starting with the lightest paint color and ending with the darkest. Allow to dry.

4. If your design was done on fabric, heat-set the design. Cover the batik piece with paper towels first, and then follow the directions in "Heat-Setting Fabric Paints" on page 14.

Experiments to Try with Crayon Batik

- Follow steps 1 and 2 for "Crayon Batik" on page 55. Applying pressure, scrape applicator-tipped paint over the crayon rubbings, using a credit card.//
- Follow the experiment above, and then stamp images onto the surface of the scraped crayon batik, using acrylic paint (see "Rubber Stamping" on page 36).

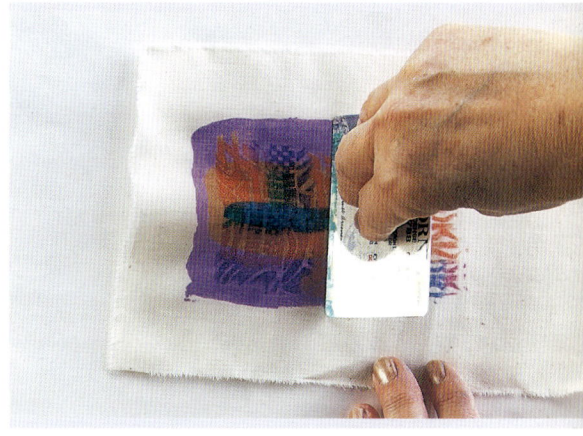

Experiment: Scraping paint over the crayon rubbings

Experiment: Rubber stamping over the crayon batik

The center of this sample was created by doing crayon rubbings on fabric. Aqua and bronze applicator-tipped paint was squeezed at the top of the rubbings and scraped over the crayon images with a credit card. Violet acrylic paint was used to stamp a figure and a row of repeat spiral designs on top of the scraped paint. Bronze applicator-tipped paint was used to highlight the figure.

TAPE RESISTS

A masking-tape resist was used to create this design. Additional color was applied with rubber stamping, washes, dry sponging, and applicator-tipped paint.

TAPE RESISTS ARE dramatic. Tape is placed on the design surface; then paint, markers, colored pencils, crayons, or other coloring agents are applied over the surface of the tape. When the tape is removed, areas of the background show through the area that was blocked with tape. You can also apply the tape to a previously painted surface and add more paint to build up the layers for rich effects.

Masking tape can be used on fabric, and drafting tape can be used on paper. Masking tape comes in a variety of widths. The widest that I have seen is 3". The wider tapes offer more possibilities, because you can cut creative shapes from them, increasing the design possibilities. You can also use medical adhesive tape as a resist on fabric. It can be removed and reapplied to another area of the design, or it can be ironed into place for a permanent element in the composition. In addition, Plaid manufactures tapes with decorative edges; look for them in craft stores.

Materials

NOTE: *Refer to the "Getting Started" section on pages 10–21 for information about painting surfaces, paints and coloring agents, tools, and other important subjects.*

- Tape: masking, drafting, medical adhesive, or decorative
- Scissors or paper edgers
- Paint surface
- Paints
- Paint palette
- Paper towels
- Sponges, flat paintbrush, old credit card, toothbrush, plastic knife, rubber stamps, and stamp pad
- Water container

Instructions

1. Using scissors or paper edgers, cut the tape into shapes, if desired, and apply them to the paint surface. You can also tear the tape.
2. Apply paint over the tape, using your preferred technique (see "Dry Sponging" on page 24, "Washes" on page 29, "Rubber Stamping" on page 36, "Applicator-Tipped Paint Techniques" on page 43, "Scraping Paint with a Credit Card" on page 47, and "Toothbrush Spatter" on page 48. Allow to dry.
3. Remove the tape.
4. Repeat steps 1–3 if desired.

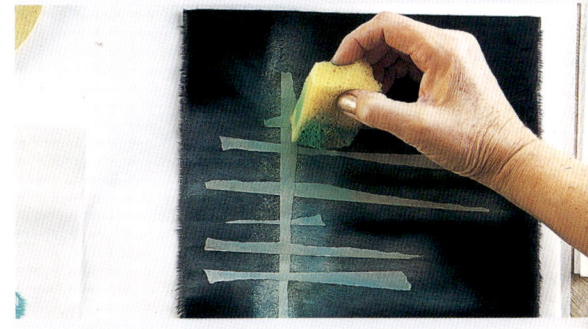

Step 2

Step 2

Step 3

In this sample, adhesive tape was used as a resist. Color was applied over the tape with washes, applicator-tipped paint, sponging, and rubber stamping. The adhesive tape was removed and then reapplied to a different spot with the help of an iron. The top and bottom borders are scrunched fabric; the side borders were sponged while the fabric was wet.

RESISTS 59

FREEZER-PAPER RESISTS

Freezer-paper resists are used in the same way as tape resists (see "Tape Resists" on page 58). Cut or tear freezer paper into any shape and iron it onto the paint surface. Apply wet paints or dry media, such as colored pencils, crayons, markers, gel rollers, ballpoint pens, oil pastels, or other coloring agents over the paint surface, then remove the freezer paper to expose the finished design. The freezer paper can be re-applied as needed. Experiment to unlock the creative possibilities of freezer paper.

Materials

NOTE: *Refer to the "Getting Started" section on pages 10–21 for information about painting surfaces, paints and coloring agents, tools, and other important subjects.*

- Freezer paper
- Paper scissors
- Iron and ironing board
- Paint surface
- Paints
- Paint palette
- Paper towels
- Sponges, flat paintbrush, old credit card, toothbrush, plastic knife, rubber stamps, and stamp pads as desired for applying paint
- Water container

Instructions

1. Cut or tear freezer paper into the desired design. Iron the freezer paper onto the paint surface.
2. Follow steps 2 and 3 on page 59 for "Tape Resists," substituting the freezer paper for the tape.
3. Repeat as desired.

A freezer-paper resist with a rubber-stamped image was used to create this sample. The background was rubber stamped and sponged. I used dry sponging and washes for some of the colored areas. The borders were created with rubber stamps and washes.

Freezer-Paper Blocks for Rubber Stamps

It's easy to create blocks for rubber stamps. Freezer paper works well to block out the paint on fabric or paper. Tapes and Con-Tact paper can also be used to make a block for an image stamped on fabric. Place masking or drafting tape over a stamped image. The tape is translucent, which makes it possible to use a permanent marker to trace the image onto the tape. Remove the tape, cut out the design, and place it back over the stamped image. Stamp or sponge over the tape-blocked image. Remove the tape when finished.

Materials

NOTE: *Refer to the "Getting Started" section on pages 10–21 for information about painting surfaces, paints and coloring agents, tools, and other important subjects.*

- Materials for "Freezer-Paper Resists" on page 60
- Rubber stamps and stamp pads
- Sponge

Instructions

1. Rubber stamp an image onto the paint surface (see "Rubber Stamping" on page 36).
2. Stamp the same image onto the dull side of a piece of freezer paper. Cut out the freezer-paper image with paper scissors.
3. Iron the freezer-paper image onto the rubber-stamped image on your paint surface.
4. Print rubber-stamp patterns over the freezer-paper edges and in the area around them.
5. Sponge around the outer edges of the freezer-paper block (see "Sponge Painting" on page 22). Remove the freezer paper.

Step 2

Step 3

Step 4

Step 5

GELS AND MODELING-PASTE RESISTS

Modeling paste on black fabric was used to create this sample. A deeply etched rubber stamp applied in a repeat pattern created the texture. The lighter rows of color are the original brushed modeling paste on the surface. The adjacent darker rows are imprints made on the cloth after pressing the stamp into the wet paste. After drying, each strip was colored with metallic paint applied by dry brushing. The borders were created with textured brayers on the black fabric.

WONDERFUL GELS AND modeling pastes are available from craft and art stores. When dry, they provide an incredible textured surface to paint. They can be applied with or without color. If you wish to color the gels or modeling pastes, use acrylic paint or permanent inks to color them before adhering them to the paint surface. After they are dry, additional paint colors can be applied to the dry surface. The highlights can be painted with a dry brush or sponge.

All textural mediums can be textured with unmounted, deeply etched rubber stamps, grids, screens, kitchen tools, nails, tissue paper, paper towels, sequin waste, stiff brushes, or any other object that can create texture. This is a technique that invites experimentation since each texturing tool will yield different results. Keep a record for reference in creating future projects.

Materials

NOTE: *Refer to the "Getting Started" section on pages 10–21 for information about painting surfaces, paints and coloring agents, tools, and other important subjects.*

- Golden molding paste or Liquitex modeling paste in various consistencies, or Golden heavy-bodied gel medium
- Paint surface
- Wide, flat brush
- Deeply etched, unmounted rubber stamps, grids, or other dimensional objects
- Acrylic paints
- Paint palette
- Paper towels
- Sponges (optional)
- Water container

Step 1

Instructions

1. Add acrylic paint to color the modeling paste or gel if desired. Apply the modeling paste or gel to the paint surface, using a wide, flat brush. The paste or gel should be about $1/16$" thick—if you use more paste or gel, it might be difficult to obtain impressions. Try different thicknesses and see which works best for your desired effect.

2. Press deeply etched rubber stamps, grids, or other dimensional objects into the paste or gel; remove and repeat as desired. If using stamps, each time the stamp is removed, stamp the excess paste or gel onto another area of the paint surface for additional interest.

3. Let the textural surface dry. Apply a colored wash to the surface of the texture, using a brush or sponge (see "Washes" on page 29).

4. Emphasize the raised areas of the texture by applying acrylic paint to the textured area with a *dry* brush. To do this, dip the brush into paint and brush the excess onto a paper towel. Apply the paint in layers, building rich color with many applications of paint. Metallic paints are especially effective.

Step 2

Step 4

RESISTS

PRINTMAKING WITHOUT A PRESS

Simple printmaking techniques make it possible to create **wonderful** pieces with minimal cost and little effort. This section will cover many techniques that use items **easily** found in most homes. Once you try the techniques, **explore** other ways to make "prints." Making a print is nothing more than placing paint on an item and then "printing" it onto a surface. That means that almost **anything** can become a printing tool. Going through kitchen drawers will yield wonderful items to print with.

EASY PRINTMAKING TECHNIQUES involve cutting potatoes into shapes, applying paint to them, and then printing with them. With that concept in mind, imagine all of the incredible possibilities for applying paint to a surface with items you never considered using. This is definitely one of those "what if?" situations. Experiment and take notes on your findings for future reference.

MONOPRINTS

THE WORD *monoprint* means one print, but it's possible to get more than one print, depending upon how much paint is applied to the printing surface. Any slick surface can be used for this technique, but I prefer using the coated side of freezer paper. Sheets of plastic, glass, metal, or any other smooth surfaces will also work for monoprinting. I like the ease of cleanup with freezer paper, so it's the best tool for my printing needs. You can print on any surface, but dark surfaces are very dramatic, especially when using metallic paints.

This sample shows a monoprint created by scraping paint at right angles on freezer paper with an adhesive spreader and then printing it onto cloth. The side borders were rubber stamped and dry sponged. Metallic details were painted with a detail brush.

Step 1

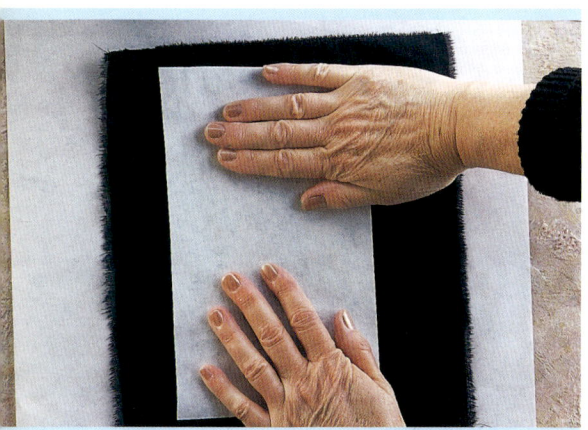

Step 2

Step 3

Materials

NOTE: *Refer to the "Getting Started" section on pages 10–21 for information about painting surfaces, paints and coloring agents, tools, and other important subjects.*

- Freezer paper
- Scissors
- Paint surface
- Paints
- Sponges
- Old credit card
- Multi-use adhesive spreader with notched edges (available at hardware and paint stores)
- Paper towels
- Water container

Instructions

1. Cut a piece of freezer paper that is slightly smaller than the paint surface. Roll the freezer paper several times in the opposite direction of the curl to flatten it before working. Squeeze one or more paint colors onto the shiny side of the freezer paper. Any paint can be used, but tube paint should be diluted before doing monoprints. Spread the paint out with an old credit card, a sponge, or a flat brush.

2. Turn the freezer paper facedown onto the paint surface and press evenly across the back of the freezer paper with your fingertips. If the paint is liquid, such as a dye or ink, the paint surface must be placed on top of the freezer paper.

3. Remove the freezer paper and repeat the process if desired. If there is excess paint on the freezer paper, make additional prints. You can turn wet fabric or paper onto other surfaces to make additional prints as well.

Experiments to Try with Monoprints

- Apply paint on the freezer paper with a brayer, and print.
- Apply paint to the freezer paper and use a credit card to make patterns in the paint.
- Stamp into wet paint with a rubber stamp, removing paint from the freezer paper. Print the freezer-paper design onto your paint surface.
- Lay a found object on fabric or paper before monoprinting.

STRING PRINTS

IT'S EASY TO make print blocks of any size by gluing strings onto foam-core board. For each print, use the same string thickness for even prints. Try different strings for different effects. Various patterns can be created, and these patterns can be easily printed onto a paint surface. Experiment with different patterns and swirls, and with wrapping the string around foam-core board and printing with the tops and sides. When gluing items to foam-core board, use a waterproof glue. Store your foam-core-and-string printing blocks in a resealable bag after they have dried.

Materials

NOTE: *Refer to the "Getting Started" section on pages 10–21 for information about painting surfaces, paints and coloring agents, tools, and other important subjects.*

- Foam-core board
- Craft knife and self-healing cutting mat
- Permanent marker
- Waterproof glue
- String of various thicknesses
- Paints
- Paint palette
- Scissors

Rows of string were glued to foam-core board for this sample. Three colors of paint were sponged onto the string and printed on the paint surface. The right border was created with rubber stamping and a wash. The left border was created with layers of sponged color and printed with grids.

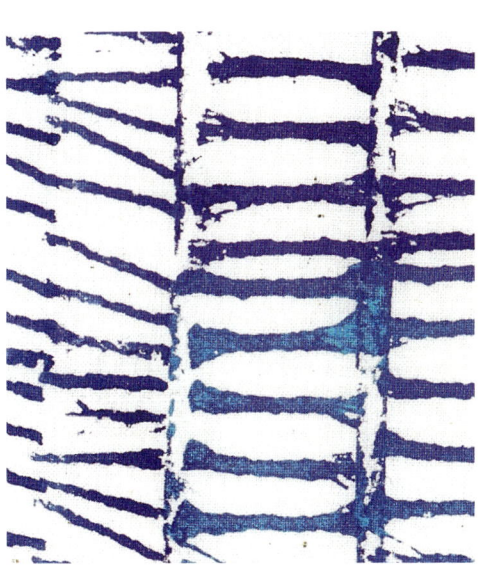

Materials (continued)

- Sponges
- Paint surface
- Paper towels
- Water container
- Resealable plastic bags

Instructions

1. Cut a piece of foam-core board to the size desired, using a craft knife and a self-healing mat. Draw a design with a permanent marker on the foam-core board.

2. Squeeze a 1½" line of waterproof glue on the marked line. Place the string on the line and continue applying glue and string until the design line is covered. Let the glue dry.

3. Apply paint to the string design, using a sponge. Print the image onto the paint surface. Repeat as desired.

4. Let paint surface dry; store foam-core blocks in resealable plastic bags.

Step 3

BUBBLE-WRAP PRINTS

This sample shows metallic paint applied with two different sizes of bubble wrap onto a dark surface. The narrow center band was done with brayers and rubber stamping.

PRINTING WITH BUBBLE wrap in various sizes makes a wonderful surface. Experiment with different sizes and shapes for this very easy technique.

Materials

NOTE: *Refer to the "Getting Started" section on pages 10–21 for information about painting surfaces, paints and coloring agents, tools, and other important subjects.*

- Paints
- Paint palette
- Bubble wrap
- Sponges
- Paint surface
- Paper towels
- Water container

Step 2

Instructions

1. Apply one or more paint colors to bubble wrap with a sponge. Turn the bubble wrap facedown onto the paint surface.

2. Press the back of the bubble wrap to transfer the paint to the surface. Remove bubble wrap. Repeat as desired.

FOAM-PLATE PRINTS

This sample was made with animal shapes cut from a Styrofoam plate. The animal shapes on the top of the sample were printed in three colors on a dark background. Two different triangular designs were created and printed alternately on the bottom of the sample. The whole process took less than forty-five minutes to complete.

FOAM-PLATE PRINTING IS one of my students' favorite techniques. It's easy to do and offers endless design possibilities. The results are so stunning that creating more than one print will be the rule rather than the

exception. Try a variety of foam plates, butcher's trays, containers, cups, or any other foam items you find. Each will make slightly different lines on a surface. The process is incredibly simple. The plate image can be used for a number of prints but will eventually break down. I do not wash it between printings. If the piece breaks down, create another one.

Materials

NOTE: *Refer to the "Getting Started" section on pages 10–21 for information about painting surfaces, paints and coloring agents, tools, and other important subjects.*

- Foam plate or plastic container
- Craft scissors
- Paper edgers (optional)
- Ballpoint pen
- Paint surface
- Paints
- Paint palette
- Sponges
- Paper towels
- Water container

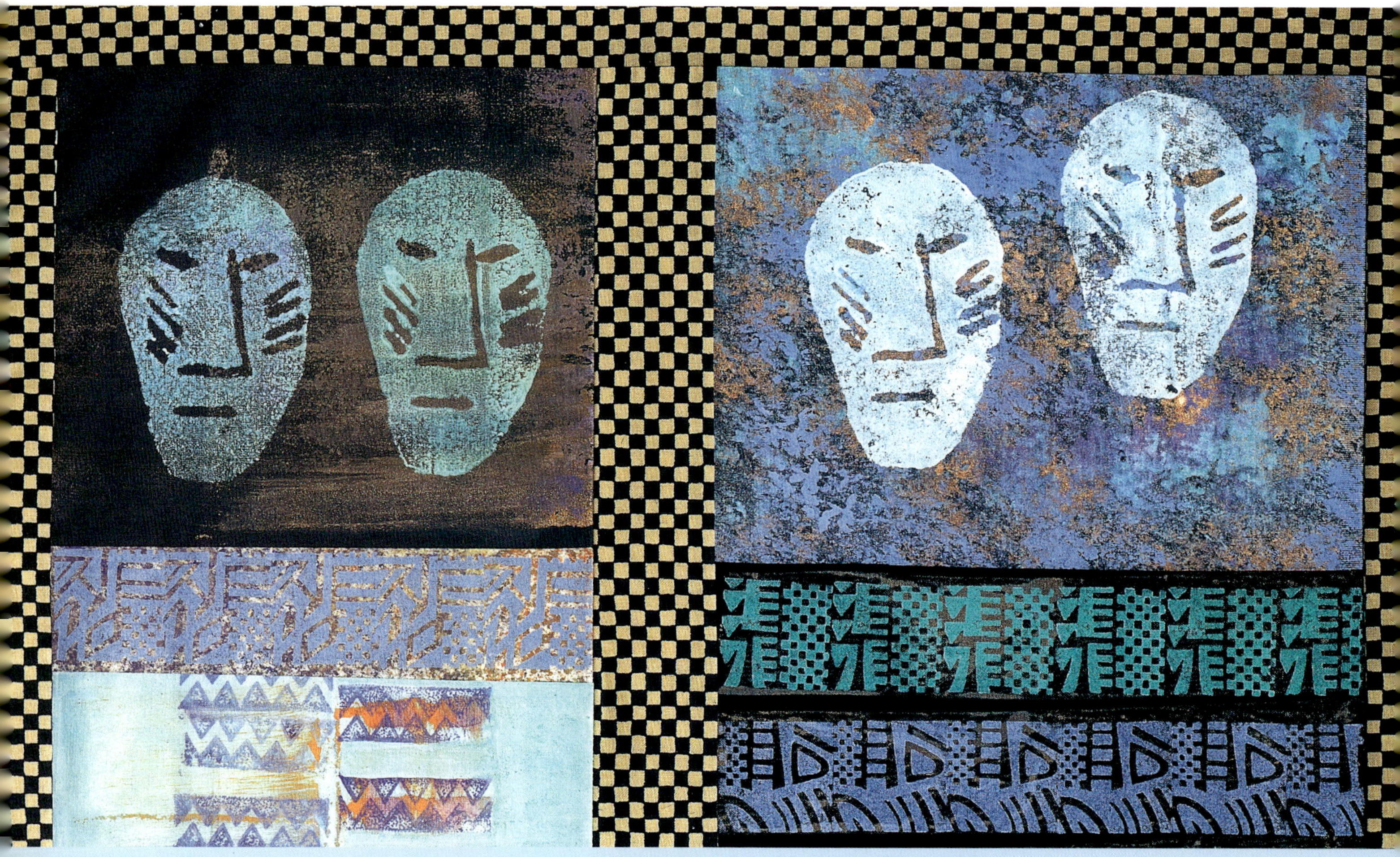

The sample above shows dark masks printed on a light, multicolored background. Below left, light masks are printed on a prepainted dark background. The sample below right was done by printing two light mask prints on a sponged multicolored background. Rubber stamping was added to the designs.

Instructions

1. Plan a design on paper, or work free-form on the foam. Cut the foam to the size and shape desired. It can be as small as a postage stamp or as large as the size of a lid on a disposable container. Cut the edges of the design with craft scissors or paper edgers.

2. If you planned your design on paper, draw the design on the foam with a ballpoint pen. Press hard with the ballpoint pen to score the lines into the surface.

3. Sponge paint onto the design. Turn the foam image over and press it onto the paint surface to make a print. Remove foam. Repeat as desired.

Step 2

Experiments to Try with Foam-Plate Printing

- Cut free-form shapes, such as animals, leaves, dolls, or petroglyphs.
- Print on prepainted backgrounds.
- Cut the design with a paper edger that creates scalloped or other decorative edges like those on a postage stamp, and create tiny images for printing and repeat patterns.
- Cut the middle of the design away and rubber stamp in the opening, or leave it empty.
- Make repeat patterns with shapes that connect.
- Combine prints with other painting techniques.

Step 3

PRINTMAKING WITHOUT A PRESS

COMBINING THE TECHNIQUES

The key to any **creative** process is to constantly **explore** the **possibilities.** There is no single answer to the creative process. The **mood** you're in, the music that's playing, and the way you feel all **influence** the final product. Constantly ask yourself **"What if?"** and let yourself be led down many creative paths.

ACHIEVING A RICH, textured, painted surface is as simple as applying layers of paint with a variety of techniques, such as rubber stamping, washes, sponging, and highlighting with applicator-tipped paint. Adding other techniques can create even more complex surfaces. Refer to the technique instructions throughout this book for more ideas. Changing one step in the layering process changes the finished design. Switching steps also results in the final piece being dramatically different.

CREATING A RICH PAINTED SURFACE IN FIVE EASY STEPS

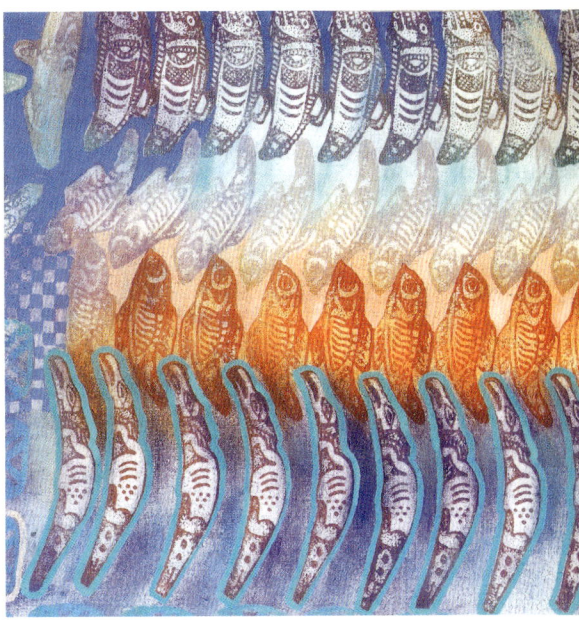

This sample shows rubber stamping, washes, and dry sponging combined to create a rich painted surface.

Materials

NOTE: *Refer to the "Getting Started" section on pages 10–21 for information about painting surfaces, paints and coloring agents, tools, and other important information.*

- Rubber stamps and stamp pads
- Paint surface
- Paints
- Paint palette
- Sponges
- Paper towels
- Water container
- Applicator-tipped paint

Instructions

1. Stamp one or more images on the selected surface (see "Rubber Stamping" on page 36). Allow the surface to dry.

2. Apply a light wash over the rubber-stamped areas with a sponge (see "Washes" on page 29). Repeat with additional colors, if desired; allow to dry.

Step 1

Step 2

Step 3

Step 4

Step 5

3. Sponge textural areas onto the paint surface (see "Sponge Painting" on page 22); allow to dry.

4. Stamp images over the washed and sponged areas; allow to dry. Add more sponging if desired; allow to dry.

5. Highlight selected areas with applicator-tipped paint (see page 43); allow to dry.

6. Repeat steps 1–5 as desired.

This sample combines rubber stamping, appliqué of dyed commercial rayon ribbon, rubber-stamped ribbon, applicator-tipped paint, metallic thread lines, sponging, and computer-generated fabric collage.

This sample combines rubber stamping, crayon rubbing, washable- and permanent-marker lines, gel-roller lines, ballpoint-pen lines, washes, separate rubber-stamped pieces glued to the surface, and applicator-tipped-paint details.

COMBINING THE TECHNIQUES

GALLERY

BOXES

Left: This box was created with painted fabric sewn over mat board. A book in the shape of a figure accompanies the box.

Bottom left: This box was created by collaging cardboard with paper and painting it. A hot-melt glue piece that was stamped and painted decorates the top of the box.

Bottom right: A cardboard box covered with sponged paint, rubber stamping, and collage. The lid is decorated with raffia and clay that was rubber stamped, painted, and impressed.

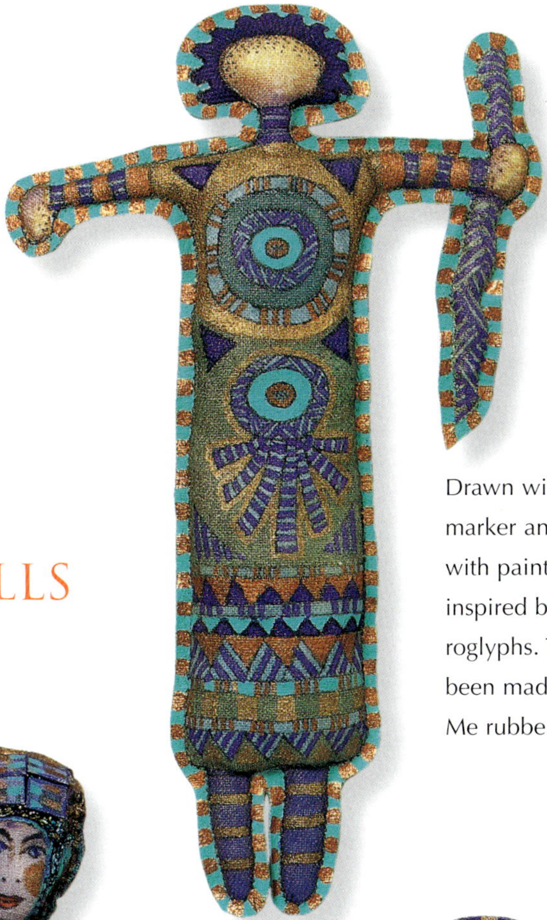

DOLLS

Drawn with a permanent marker and then decorated with paint, this doll was inspired by Southwest petroglyphs. The image has been made into an Impress Me rubber stamp.

Drawn with a permanent marker and then decorated with paint, this doll is based on a photo of an Eskimo. The image has been made into an Impress Me rubber stamp.

A doll that was drafted with a permanent marker and then decorated with paint and beads. This original design has been made into an Impress Me rubber stamp.

This doll was stamped with an Impress Me rubber stamp and then painted and decorated with beads and yarn.

GALLERY 77

BOOKS

Above left: This book was rubber stamped, painted, and decorated with a metal-embossed piece. The pages were stapled together.

Above right: This book was rubber stamped, painted, and closed with braided yarn and a button made from Play-Doh. Two shrink-plastic dangles hang from the braided yarn. The book was stapled together.

Left: This book was decorated with brayer-painted paper, seed beads, and rubber stamping. A band with a hot-melt glue decoration closes the book. The book was bound with cord and beads.

Above: This book was decorated with stamped impressions plus sponging and collaged embossed triangles. Raffia was used to bind the book.

Right: This book was created with painted fabric that had been quilted, decorated with additional paint, and rubber stamped. Beads and rubber stamp–impressed Super Sculpey embellish the book. It was bound with cord and beads.

Below: This book was decorated with a print made from a foam lid. Rubber-stamped impressions border the print. Raffia was used to bind the book.

GALLERY 79

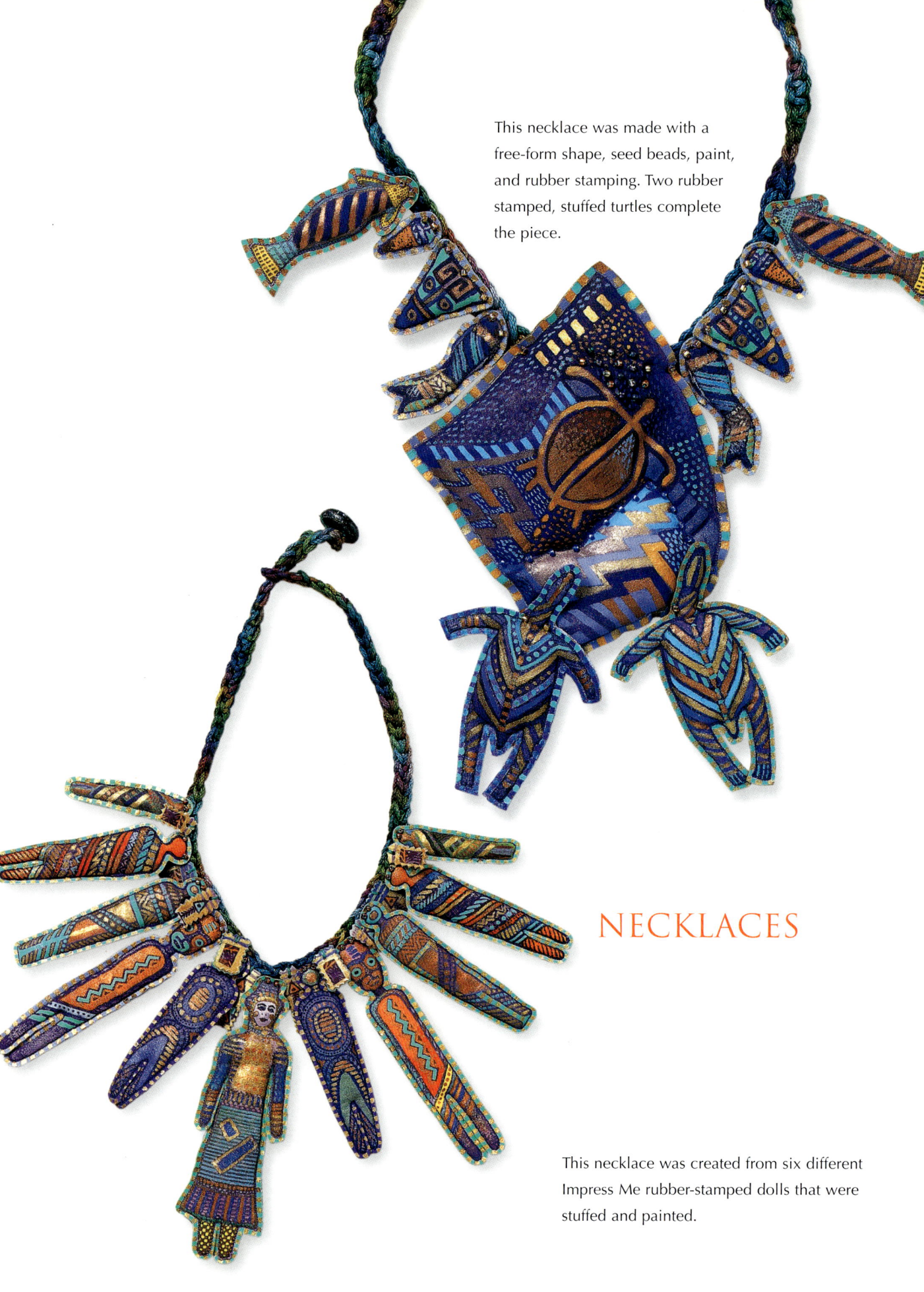

This necklace was made with a free-form shape, seed beads, paint, and rubber stamping. Two rubber stamped, stuffed turtles complete the piece.

NECKLACES

This necklace was created from six different Impress Me rubber-stamped dolls that were stuffed and painted.

VESTS

Above: This vest was created by scrunching wet silk that had been painted with Dr. Ph. Martin's ReadyTex paint. After the vest pieces were dry and heat-set, rubber stamping was applied with Jacquard Lumiere metallic paint. The stripes were painted with Dr. Ph. Martin's ReadyTex metallic paint, using a small, flat brush. Some of the rubber stamps were outlined with Jacquard Lumiere paint and a small brush.

Right: For this vest, black fabric was covered with rubber stamping, sponging, masking tape resist, painted shapes, and applicator-tipped paint.

GALLERY 81

GLASS, CERAMIC, AND PLASTIC ART PIECES

A white ceramic plate was sponged and rubber stamped with Delta's Perm Enamel. The details were painted with a small, flat brush.

Right: This plastic touch light was painted and stamped with Pebeo's Vitrea glass paint. The base was sponge painted with Dr. Ph. Martin's metal craft paint.

Below: A clear glass was sponged and rubber stamped with Delta's glass paint. The details were painted with a small, flat brush.

GALLERY 83

WALL HANGINGS

Above: The fabric for this wall hanging was created with various painting and sponging techniques. Rubber stamping, foam-plate fish prints, and applicator-tipped paint complete the design.

Right: This wall hanging was created with painted and rubber-stamped fabric, applicator-tipped paint, beading, appliquéd yarn and fabric, and metallic-thread embroidery.

VEST

85

This painted vest was created with simple sponging, wet-into-wet techniques, and rubber stamping. For accent, some of the areas were highlighted with applicator-tipped paint. For best results, choose an easy commercial lined vest pattern with minimal seams. In order to match the lining to the painted vest fabric, purchase the lining after painting the fabric. Or purchase extra muslin for the lining and paint it at the same time as the vest fabric. The vest can be embellished with ribbons, cords, buttons, charms, dangling pieces, or beads.

Materials

Note: *Refer to the "Getting Started" section on pages 10–21 for information about painting surfaces, paints and coloring agents, tools, and other important subjects.*

- Simple commercial vest pattern with lining
- Vest fabric: quilter's muslin (bleached or unbleached), china silk, or plain or lightly textured fabric in any color (yardage as indicated on the pattern envelope)
- Lining fabric
- Fabric scraps (leftover vest or other fabric) for appliqués
- Acrylic paint
- Fabric paint
- Sponges
- Impress Me rubber stamps
- Jacquard Lumiere metallic acrylic paint
- Detail brush and small flat brush
- Applicator-tipped paint
- Freezer paper
- Paper towels
- Water container
- Sewing machine and sewing supplies
- Thread to match the painted vest
- Iron and ironing board

Instructions

1. Cut the vest fabric, following the pattern instructions. Apply paint to the fabric using any of the techniques in this book.

2. Rubber stamp images on some areas of the vest, using acrylic paint or jar fabric paint (see "Rubber Stamping" on page 36).

3. Sponge the fabric with Lumiere acrylics, jar acrylic paint, or craft acrylic paint (see "Sponge Painting" on page 22)

4. Cut small rectangular pieces and narrow strips from leftover vest fabric or other scraps. Paint if desired, using one of the techniques in this book. Appliqué the fabric pieces to the vest sections as desired, using a machine straight stitch or zigzag stitch.

5. Paint details on the vest with a detail brush or with a small, flat brush.

6. Use applicator-tipped paint to highlight selected areas (see "Applicator-Tipped Paint Techniques" on page 43).

7. Repeat steps 2–6 as needed.

8. Assemble the vest according to the pattern instructions.

Step 5

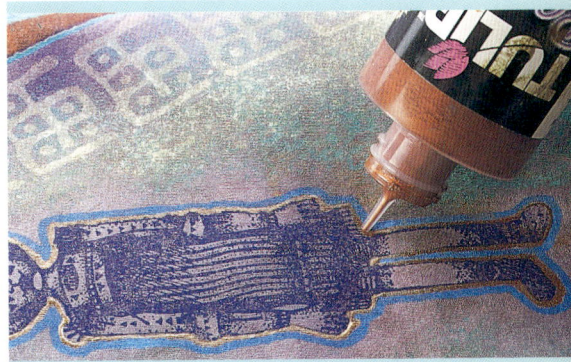

Step 6

DOLL

THIS DOLL WAS created using an angel-doll image from Impress Me rubber-stamp set 71. After stamping the image, it was sewn, stuffed, and embellished. This technique can be applied to any sewn-and-stuffed piece. The same rubber stamp could be used again and again to make dolls, and each would be quite different. Colors could be changed, or embellishments such as dangles, beads, charms, embroidery, or appliqué could be added. The dolls are so much fun, make several and try a variety of ideas.

Materials

NOTE: *Refer to the "Getting Started" section on pages 10–21 for information about painting surfaces, paints and coloring agents, tools, and other important subjects.*

- ¼ yard fabric, such as muslin or printed cotton
- Acrylic paint such as Dr. Ph. Martin's Spectralite, Golden tube or jar paint, or bottled craft paint
- Sponges
- Sewing machine and open-toe embroidery foot (optional)
- Basic sewing supplies (needle, thread to match the doll, sewing scissors, ball-headed pins)
- Small, flat brush (approximately ¼")
- Polyester fiberfill or cotton balls for stuffing doll
- Stuffing tool
- Button or small decorative element
- Applicator-tipped paint (optional)
- Toothpick
- Piece of corrugated cardboard at least 4" x 8"
- Fabric glue
- Small detail brush

Instructions

1. Rubber stamp a doll image onto a piece of muslin, using acrylic paint and a sponge (see "Rubber Stamping" on page 36).

Creating a Stuffing Tool

To create a stuffing tool, cut a 14- to 16-gauge piece of wire approximately 6" long. Flatten both ends with a hammer and file them smooth, using a jewelry file or a metal nail file. This tool works wonderfully for stuffing small pieces. If the arms and legs of the doll are not too small, a commercial stuffing tool can be used.

Step 3

Step 4

2. Stamp or paint a piece of fabric for the doll backing. The fabric should be at least ½" larger than the stamped image all around. Place the stamped doll piece and the backing piece wrong sides together. Sew completely around the rubber-stamped image by machine or by hand; if sewing by machine, use a very short stitch length and an open-toe embroidery foot. If sewing by hand, use very tiny running stitches.

3. Paint full-strength acrylic paint to at least ¼" from the edge of the stitching around the entire doll on both front and back sides, using a flat brush.

4. Cut out the doll about ⅛" from the stitching with a sharp pair of scissors.

5. Paint the cut edges around the doll with full-strength acrylic paint in the same color that you painted around the doll. Cut tiny slits in the back of the doll at key areas, such as below the neck, at the top of the arms and legs, and at the bend of an arm to make openings for inserting the stuffing; the stuffing tool should be able to fit easily into the slits.

Creating Fabric Motifs

To create a fabric motif, stamp a small design, such as a button or small decorative element, onto a piece of quilter's muslin. Glue at least three layers of fabric together with the fabric motif on top; let the glue dry completely, then cut out the fabric motif with a very sharp pair of scissors. Put a ball-headed pin through the fabric motif. Hold the pin in your hand, and apply acrylic paint or applicator-tipped paint to the raw edge of the motif with a toothpick to seal the edge. Stick the pin into a piece of corrugated cardboard to dry.

6. Stuff the doll with polyester fiberfill or cotton balls, using the stuffing tool. To stuff the doll easily, use tiny amounts of stuffing and push firmly with the stuffing tool. Start with the arms, legs, and head; then stuff toward the middle of the doll. Be patient; stuff slowly and *firmly*.

7. Cover the stuffing slits by gluing decorative fabric motifs in place (see "Creating Fabric Motifs" above).

8. Leave the painted seam allowances around the doll a solid color, or paint decorative checkerboards or lines on the seam allowances on both sides of the doll. Paint details on the doll with acrylic paint and a small detail brush. Make and glue additional fabric motifs to the front of the doll if desired.

9. Embellish the doll further with charms, beads, ribbons, yarn, buttons, or other decorative elements if desired.

Step 6

Step 7

WALL HANGING

IT IS VERY easy to use painted fabric in a small wall hanging. The techniques shown in this project can be used for creating garments, large quilts, place mats, decorative items for the home, book covers, or any other creative endeavor that you wish to pursue. Try a variety of color combinations, combining painted and commercial fabric, and adding embellishments.

Materials

NOTE: *Refer to the "Getting Started" section on pages 10–21 for information about painting surfaces, paints and coloring agents, tools, and other important subjects.*

- Materials for "Creating a Rich Painted Surface in Five Easy Steps" on page 73
- ½ yard quilter's muslin
- 11" x 19½" rectangle of fabric for pieced front
- 11" x 19½" rectangle of lining fabric
- Sewing machine
- Basic sewing supplies
- Point turner
- Iron and ironing board
- Fiskars rotary cutter and self-healing cutting mat with grid lines
- Acrylic grid ruler
- Piece of wood molding to place at the top of the finished wall hanging
- Medium grade sandpaper
- Quick Grab glue
- Sawtooth hanger and 2 small brads
- Hammer

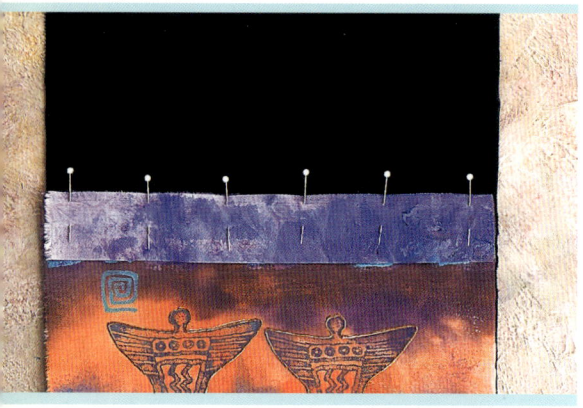

Step 2

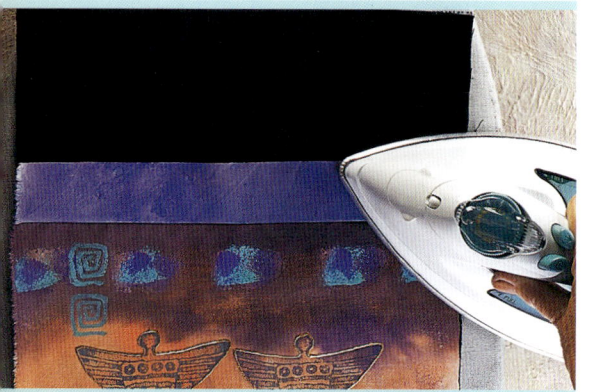

Step 3

Instructions

1. Cut a piece of muslin 10¾" x 11" for the center panel of the wall hanging. Paint the fabric, using any of the techniques in this book. Cut 1 rectangle 9" x 11" and 2 rectangles 3" x 11", and paint as desired, using the techniques in this book. Allow the pieces to dry; heat-set, following the directions on page 00. From the 9" x 11" rectangle, cut 1 strip, 4¼" x 11", and 1 strip, 3½" x 11". From each of the remaining rectangles, cut 2 strips, 1½" x 11".

2. Place the center panel onto the flannel 4" from the lower short end. Place 1 of the 1½"-wide strips on the upper edge of the center panel, right sides together, matching the upper raw edges; pin.

3. Stitch ¼" from the raw edges. Flip the strip to the right side and press well.

4. Stitch the remaining 1½"-wide fabric strip to the lower edge of the center panel in the same manner as the first strip. Stitch the 4¼"-wide strip to the top and the 3½"-wide strip to the bottom of the pieced unit in the same way; the flannel should be completely covered with painted fabric strips. Baste ¼" from the raw edges of the pieced panel.

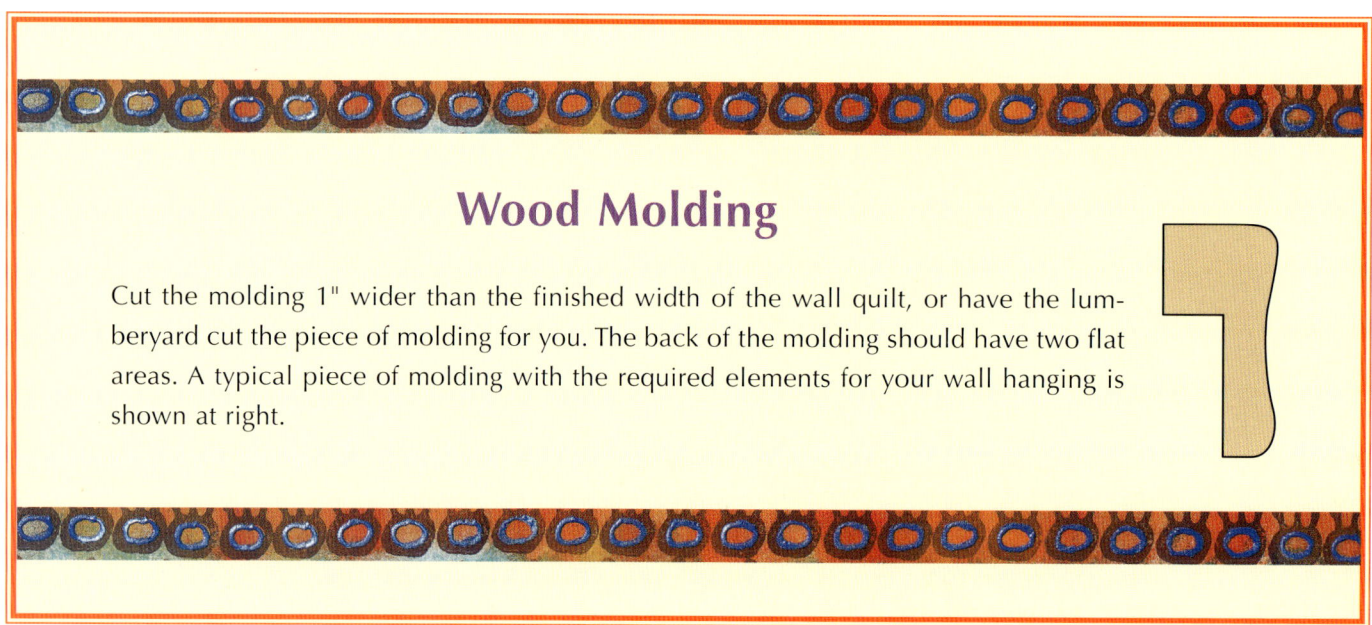

Wood Molding

Cut the molding 1" wider than the finished width of the wall quilt, or have the lumberyard cut the piece of molding for you. The back of the molding should have two flat areas. A typical piece of molding with the required elements for your wall hanging is shown at right.

5. Cut the lining the same size as the pieced panel. Place the lining and the pieced panel right sides together and pin around 3 sides. Sew ½" from the raw edges, leaving a 9" opening at the upper edge for turning. Clip the corners. Trim the seam allowances to ¼" and turn the piece to the right side through the opening; use a point turner for crisp corners. Turn the seam allowances at the opening to the inside; press and pin into place. Slipstitch the opening closed.

6. Sand the piece of molding and paint it with a sponge and acrylic paint (see "Sponge Painting" on page 22). Multiple colors can be sponged onto the wood to coordinate it with the wall hanging. Paint both the back and the front of the molding.

7. Rubber stamp designs in coordinating colors onto the painted piece of wood (see "Rubber Stamping" on page 36).

8. Turn the molding piece over. Apply glue to the flat, recessed area of the molding. Center the upper edge of the wall hanging over the molding strip, front side down; press into the glue. Let the glue dry. Attach the sawtooth hanger with 2 brads to the top center back of the molding, using a hammer.

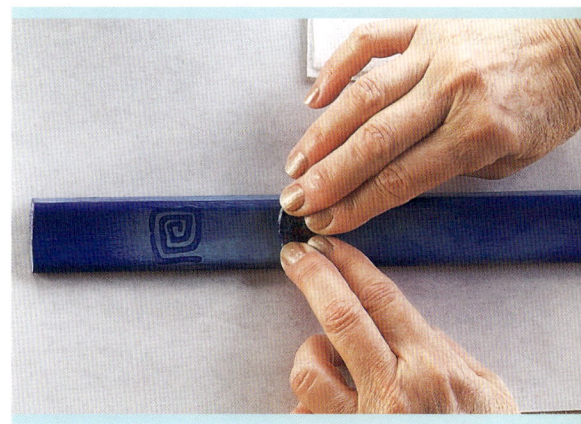

Step 7

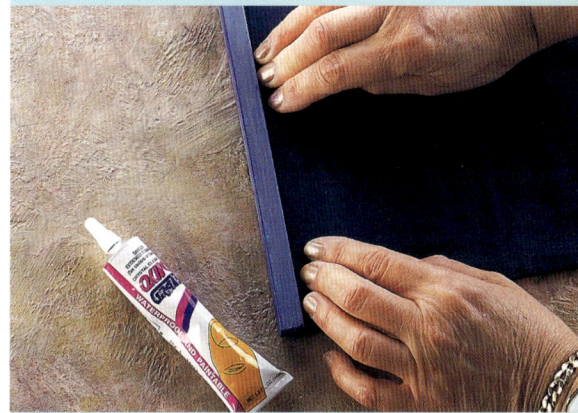

Step 8

Embellish the Wall Hanging

Make the wall hanging more interesting by adding fabric motifs (see "Creating Fabric Motifs" on page 91), beads, buttons, ribbons, dangles, yarn, decorative threads, cords, raw-edge appliqué, embroidery stitches, machine embroidery, or seed beads to the design. Be sure to add any embellishments before you attach the lining.

JOURNAL

THIS JOURNAL IS quite easy to make. Its versatility and ease of construction make it great fun for all ages. Try different cover-weight papers and different paper for the interior pages when creating your journal. The interior pages can be as simple as typing paper, or you can use beautiful specialty papers, such as rice paper or handmade paper. Because the binding is so flexible, any number of pages can be placed in the book. The only limitation to the thickness of the book is the length of the brass paper fastener you use.

Materials

NOTE: *Refer to the "Getting Started" section on pages 10–21 for information about painting surfaces, paints and coloring agents, tools, and other important subjects.*

- 2 sheets of cover-weight (at least 60 pounds) paper or card stock
- Paper for interior pages of journal
- Pencil
- Ruler, steel-edged
- Rotary cutter and self-healing cutting mat with grid lines
- Sponges
- Impress Me rubber stamps
- Acrylic paints
- Fiskars ⅛" hole punch
- Brass fasteners in any size (found in stationery-supply stores)
- Ballpoint pen or ball-headed tool for scoring

Instructions

1. Cut a piece of cover-weight paper to the desired width and height of the finished book; this will be the front cover. Cut a second piece of cover-weight paper the same height as the first piece and about 3" wider for the back cover of the book.

2. Decorate the front and back covers with sponge painting (see page 22), rubber stamping (see page 36), alternative tools (see page 42), or resists (see page 54).

Step 2

JOURNAL 97

Not Just for the Deli

Sandwich paper makes wonderful interior pages for journals (see "Paper" on page 11). Sandwich paper that has been placed under painting projects to cover a work surface is often quite gorgeous and can be reused. Choose the most interesting pieces of painted sandwich paper and leave them as is, or sponge a metallic wash over them to create gorgeous paper for book pages. Because sandwich paper is water-resistant, it is strong and can accommodate washes without buckling easily.

Step 5

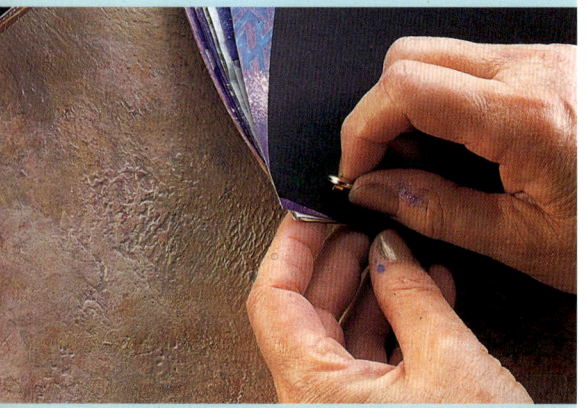

Step 6

3. Cut the interior pages of the book slightly smaller than the front cover. Measure carefully and cut 2 or 3 pages at a time, using a metal-edged ruler and a rotary cutter on a self-healing cutting mat.

4. Measure 2 spots 1" from the long edges of the back cover and ½" from 1 short edge of the cover; punch ⅛" holes at the marked spots, using a hole punch.

5. Place the shorter front cover under the longer back cover and align short edges on the left side. Use a pencil to mark the holes for the front cover; punch the holes with the hole punch. Lay the book pages, one by one, under the back cover, aligning the left edges of the pages with the left edge of the cover. Mark the pages for holes on the left sides of the book pages. Punch the holes in 2 or 3 interior pages at a time at the marked spots.

6. Place the front cover, right side up, on top of the interior pages of the book. Place the longer back cover on top, right side down, aligning all the holes on the left sides. Insert a brass fastener through each set of holes. Flatten the prongs on the back cover of the book.

7. Draw a line on the wrong side of the back cover of the book, 1" from the edge with the brass fasteners, using a ballpoint pen or scoring tool. Fold on the marked line to crease. On the wrong side of the back cover, mark and fold a second crease line 1" from the first line.

   If the book is thicker than ¼", measure the depth of the book and mark a parallel line that distance away from the second line; fold to make a third crease line if necessary. Fold on all the crease lines and roll the back cover to the back of the book. There will now be a finished edge on the left front side of the book to cover the brass fasteners. If the back cover extends beyond the front cover and you wish to trim the covers to match, use a rotary cutter and a steel-edged ruler on a self-healing cutting mat.

8. Rubber stamp or decorate the folded edge of the book, using one of the painting techniques in this book.

Step 7

Step 8

Cutting Paper for the Journal

Mark the cutting lines for the covers and the pages with a pencil. Place one cover sheet on a self-healing mat. Make sure that the edge of the paper aligns with the grid markings. Place a metal ruler across the paper along the grid lines. Always cut into the waste side when cutting the paper. Cut the paper by placing a rotary-cutter blade next to the ruler and rolling away from the bottom edge toward the top edge of the paper. Since paper dulls the rotary-cutter blades, keep a special blade to use only for paper. Cut the second cover sheet 3" wider than the first.

WOOD FRAME

ALL OF THE painting techniques in this book work beautifully on wood. Always use acrylic paints for any projects that cannot be heat-set. Any acrylic paint will work and can be applied by sponging, brushing, or rubber stamping.

Materials

NOTE: *Refer to the "Getting Started" section on pages 10–12 for information about painting surfaces, paints and coloring agents, tools, and other important subjects.*

- Unfinished wood frame
- Acrylic paints
- Paint palette
- Sponges
- ½"-wide flat brush
- Impress Me rubber stamps
- Paper towels
- Water container

Instructions

1. Apply paint to the wood frame using a sponge (see "Sponge Painting" on page 22). If necessary, touch up unpainted areas with the flat brush.

2. Rubber stamp images on the frame front (see "Rubber Stamping" on page 36).

3. Repeat steps 1 and 2 as desired.

Step 2

CERAMIC MUG

You can use any of the painting techniques in this book on ceramic. Different ceramic paints have different properties, so read the manufacturer's instructions before using each paint. Once cured, many of the pieces are dishwasher-safe. Any glazed piece of plain ceramic, either white or colored, can be painted. Don't be afraid to experiment. Painting ceramic pieces is great fun and can be done by all ages. If the ceramic piece is to hold food or drinks, be sure to use a paint that is intended for this purpose.

Materials

NOTE: *Refer to the "Getting Started" section on pages 10–21 for information about painting surfaces, paints and coloring agents, tools, and other important subjects.*

- Ceramic paints, such as Delta's Perm Enamel, Pebeo's Porcelaine 150, Deco Art's Ultra Gloss, and Plaid's Apple Barrel Gloss Enamel
- Paint palette
- Sponges
- Plain ceramic piece
- Paper towels
- Impress Me rubber stamps
- Detail brush

Instructions

1. Using ceramic paint, sponge color onto the ceramic piece (see "Sponge Painting" on page 22); cover the entire surface or leave some areas plain for rubber stamping in the next step.
2. Make rubber-stamped impressions (see "Rubber Stamping" on page 36) over the sponged areas or on plain areas of the ceramic piece.
3. Repeat steps 1 and 2 as desired. Paint details with a small detail brush. Follow the manufacturer's directions for finishing and curing.

Step 2

GLASS

Glass is as easy as ceramic to paint. Glasses come in interesting shapes and sizes. If the glass piece is intended for use with food, buy paint that is suitable for contact with food. Experiment with different techniques and paints for different results. This project is suitable for all age groups.

Materials

NOTE: *Refer to the "Getting Started" section on pages 10–21 for information about painting surfaces, paints and coloring agents, tools, and other important subjects.*

- Glass paints, such as Delta's Textured Gel and Transparent Glass paint, Pebeo's Vitrea, and Plaid's Gallery Glass
- Paint palette
- Sponge
- Plain glass piece
- Impress Me rubber stamps
- Paper towels
- Detail brush
- Water container

Instructions

1. Sponge color onto the glass (see "Sponge Painting" on page 22).
2. Rubber stamp over the sponged color (see "Rubber Stamping" on page 36).
3. Add details as desired with a small detail brush.
4. Repeat steps 1–3 as desired.

Step 2

GLASS 105

METAL BASKET

METAL OBJECTS ARE very easy to paint. Any metal piece can be painted using the techniques shown in this book. Metal decorator items from the craft store are wonderful to paint and embellish. Use paints especially designed for painting on metal, and prime the metal surface before painting, if necessary, following the paint manufacturer's recommendations.

Materials

NOTE: *Refer to the "Getting Started" section on pages 10–21 for information about painting surfaces, paints and coloring agents, tools, and other important subjects.*

- Metal paint, such as Dr. Ph. Martin's Metal Craft, Delta's Perm Enamel, Deco Art's Ultra Gloss, and Plaid's Indoor and Outdoor Gloss paint
- Paint palette
- Sponges
- Metal basket or other metal project
- Flat paintbrush
- Impress Me rubber stamps
- Paper towels
- Water container

Instructions

1. Sponge color (see "Sponge Painting" on page 22) onto the basket, layering 2 or more colors for an interesting effect. Cover the basket completely, inside and outside. Touch up areas missed with a flat brush and paint.

2. Rubber stamp impressions onto the sponged areas using rubber stamps (see "Rubber Stamping" on page 36).

3. Repeat steps 1 and 2 until satisfied with the results.

Step 2

RESOURCES

Glue

Quick Grab
PO Box 15040
Scottsdale, AZ 85267-5040
Permanent, all-purpose glue

Lighting

Ott-Lite Technology
(800) 842-8848
www.ott-lite.com
Lamps

Paints, Pens, and Coloring Agents

Createx
(800) 243-2712
www.createxcolors.com
Multisurface acrylics, permanent poster and fabric paints

Deco Art
(800) 367-3047
www.decoart.com
Americana Acrylic, Ultra Gloss, metal paint

Delta Technical Coatings, Inc.
(800) 423-4135
www.deltacrafts.com
Ceramcoat, Perm Enamel, Glass Textured Gel, Transparent Glass paint, Faux Finish Glaze Base

Duncan Enterprises
(800) 438-6226
www.duncancrafts.com
Tulip applicator-tipped paint, Tulip Ultra Soft fabric paint, Aleene's glues

Golden Artist Colors, Inc.
(607) 847-6154
www.goldenpaints.com
Acrylics, gel mediums, modeling pastes, gesso

Jones Tones
(800) 397-9667
Applicator-tipped paints

Pebeo of America
(819) 829-5012
www.pebeo.com
Porcelaine 150, Vitrea, Setacolor, Setasilk

Plaid Enterprises, Inc.
(770) 923-8200
www.plaidonline.com
Folk Art acrylic, applicator-tipped paint, Indoor and Outdoor Gloss paint, brushes, foam brayers, foam painting shapes, Gallery Glass, texturing tools, water containers, paint combs

Rupert, Gibbon and Spider, Inc.
(800) 442-0455
www.jacquardproducts.com
Jacquard Lumiere, Dye-na-Flow, Textile Colors, Pearl Ex

Salis International
(800) 843-8293
www.docmartins.com
Dr. Ph. Martin's ReadyTex paint, Spectralite liquid acrylics, Metal Paint, InkPak rubber stamp pads

Staedtler, Inc.
(818) 882-6000
info@staedtler-usa.com
Markers, colored pencils, and Gel Rollers

Paper and Paper-Related Tools

Fiskars Inc.
(715) 842-2091
www.fiskars.com
Rotary cutters, brayers, portable paper cutters, self-healing cutting mats, scissors, paper edgers, hole punches

Paper Adventures
(800) 727-0699
Decorative paper, paper crimpers, paper embossers

Rubber Stamps and Accessories

Impress Me
Sherrill and Joel Kahn
Fax and phone: (818) 788-6730
impressme@earthlink.net
www.impressmenow.com
Wholesale and retail rubber stamps (all rubber stamping in this book was done with these rubber stamps). Catalog: $5.00 (refundable on the first order)

Clearsnap
(800) 448-4862
www.clearsnap.com
Rubber stamp pads

Ranger Industries
(800) 266-1397
www.rangerink.com
Fabric paint, Heat It craft tool (heat gun), rubber stamp pads, brayers, embossing powders

Tsukineko, Inc.
(800) 769-6633
www.tsukineko.com
Fabrico rubber stamp pads for fabric, rubber stamp pads

Modeling Pastes and Gels

Col Art Americas
(800) 445-4278
www.liquitex.com
Modeling paste, paints

Golden Artist Colors, Inc.
(607) 847-6154
www.goldenpaints.com
Modeling pastes, gels, paints

ABOUT THE AUTHOR

Artist **Sherrill Kahn** has been creating award-winning drawings, paintings, and fiber-based artwork for almost forty years. Her work can be found in many private collections throughout the world.  She loves to weave, quilt, airbrush, bead, sew, knit, crochet, draw, paint, and rubber stamp. In addition, she makes creative books, innovative jewelry, and dolls; paints and decorates every surface imaginable; and constantly explores new materials and new techniques. She lives by four simple words: "Have fun," and "What if?"

Sherrill teaches across the country and loves to share the sheer joy of the creative process with her students. She packs her classes with as much information as possible, taking "What if?" to new heights.

She lives in Encino, California, with Joel, her husband of almost thirty-four years. They do everything together and he is her greatest friend and supporter. They love to travel and have been in almost every state and many countries throughout the world. After retiring from teaching in the public schools, they started a rubber stamp company, called Impress Me, in 1995, which continues to grow.

NEW AND BESTSELLING TITLES FROM

America's Best-Loved Craft & Hobby Books™

America's Best-Loved Quilt Books®

QUILTING
from That Patchwork Place®, an imprint of Martingale & Company™

Appliqué
Artful Appliqué
Colonial Appliqué
Red and Green: An Appliqué Tradition
Rose Sampler Supreme
Your Family Heritage: Projects in Appliqué

Baby Quilts
Appliqué for Baby
The Quilted Nursery
Quilts for Baby: Easy as ABC
More Quilts for Baby: Easy as ABC
Even More Quilts for Baby: Easy as ABC

Holiday Quilts
Easy and Fun Christmas Quilts
Favorite Christmas Quilts from That Patchwork Place
Paper Piece a Merry Christmas
A Snowman's Family Album Quilt
Welcome to the North Pole

Learning to Quilt
Basic Quiltmaking Techniques for:
  Borders and Bindings
  Curved Piecing
  Divided Circles
  Eight-Pointed Stars
  Hand Appliqué
  Machine Appliqué
  Strip Piecing
The Joy of Quilting
The Quilter's Handbook
Your First Quilt Book (or it should be!)

Paper Piecing
50 Fabulous Paper-Pieced Stars
A Quilter's Ark
Easy Machine Paper Piecing
Needles and Notions
Paper-Pieced Curves
Show Me How to Paper Piece

Rotary Cutting
101 Fabulous Rotary-Cut Quilts
365 Quilt Blocks a Year Perpetual Calendar
Fat Quarter Quilts
Lap Quilting Lives!
Quick Watercolor Quilts
Quilts from Aunt Amy
Spectacular Scraps
Time-Crunch Quilts

Small & Miniature Quilts
Bunnies By The Bay Meets Little Quilts
Celebrate! with Little Quilts
Easy Paper-Pieced Miniatures
Little Quilts All Through the House

CRAFTS
From Martingale & Company

300 Papermaking Recipes
The Art of Handmade Paper and Collage
The Art of Stenciling
Creepy Crafty Halloween
Gorgeous Paper Gifts
Grow Your Own Paper
Stamp with Style
Wedding Ribbonry

KNITTING
From Martingale & Company

Comforts of Home
Fair Isle Sweaters Simplified
Knit It Your Way
Simply Beautiful Sweaters
Two Sticks and a String
The Ultimate Knitter's Guide
Welcome Home: Kaffe Fassett

COLLECTOR'S COMPASS™
From Martingale & Company

20th Century Glass
'50s Decor
Barbie® Doll
Jewelry

Coming to *Collector's Compass* Spring 2001:
20th Century Dinnerware
American Coins
Movie Star Collectibles
'60s Decor

Our books are available at bookstores and your favorite craft, fabric, yarn, and antiques retailers. If you don't see the title you're looking for, visit us at **www.martingale-pub.com** or contact us at:

1-800-426-3126
International: 1-425-483-3313
Fax: 1-425-486-7596
E-mail: info@martingale-pub.com

For more information and a full list of our titles, visit our Web site or call for a free catalog.